Success
with
IEPs

Lessons Learned from Implementing the Middle School Model

By Santo Piño and Dena Hook
Foreword by John H. Lounsbury

Incentive Publications, Inc.
Nashville, Tennessee

Cover by Rebecca Rüegger
Edited by Jill Norris
Copy Edited by Cary Grayson

ISBN 0-86530-051-8

1   2   3   4   5   6   7   8   9   10   09   08   07   06

PRINTED IN THE UNITED STATES OF AMERICA
www.incentivepublications.com

Table of Contents

Foreword

Public education, America's largest single enterprise, is always in flux, but never more so than in the last few decades. During these years American education has seen several major movements or developments vastly alter the way public education is conducted.

The No Child Left Behind Act of 2002 (NCLB) has brought a new dimension to public education. While having a universally desired objective, this single piece of federal legislation has created havoc in a way never before experienced. The impact of NCLB is greatest at the middle level, for the "make or break" tests in mathematics and reading occur at the fifth- and eighth-grade levels. And here where individual differences and diversity are greatest, the mismatch between NCLB's arbitrary and uniform requirements and the realities of human growth and development is most obvious and difficult—especially as it applies to students with special needs.

In this volume, educators will find both a needed perspective and just plain good advice. With passion and practicality, the authors provide important understandings about the middle school, interspersed with specific guides for operating effectively so educators can work their way through the minefield that special education has become in the heyday of No Child Left Behind. The authors are bona fide experts; they know whereof they speak, and in this engaging two-dimensional presentation they provide advice on how to successfully differentiate instruction in keeping with the new interpretations in IDEA 2004 that more specifically relate to academic achievement.

The engaging and personal presentations of the authors make it clear that special education and the middle school movement grow out of the same foundations, with philosophies that are compatible. Because of their natural child-centered bent, middle school teachers have been commendably successful in working with like-minded special education teachers to make inclusion work for the benefit of all students. With this new resource, advocates of both specialties have a new tool to help develop successful Individualized Educational Programs.

– John H. Lounsbury

About This Book

The coauthors of this book have been involved with the education of special needs children for the last 20 years.

> *Dena Hook* is a parent/advocate for children with special needs. She works on behalf of these children to assure that school districts provide the proper services to meet the needs of individual students. She brings to this writing two unique perspectives: one as a parent of a child with a disability, and another as a professional trainer and advocate for children with special needs. She continues to examine school practices from both parents' and advocates' perspectives.

> *Dr. Santo H. Piño* is a middle school principal and director. He has spent the last 15 years designing and operating two middle schools built on an inclusion model. Dr. Piño speaks from the perspective of a principal and program director of middle school programs. His efforts are focused on building inclusion practices for all children in middle school settings, regardless of their needs.

In each chapter, the authors will present their comments and suggestions from their own particular perspectives. Both viewpoints reinforce the concept that when parents and school systems work together collaboratively, schools become the learning environments all children need and, most importantly, deserve.

This book provides an overview of their collective experiences and demonstrates how working together in a collaborative non-adversarial partnership, utilizing a properly implemented middle school model of inclusive education, can maximize the educational experience for all students.

Chapter 1

An Educator's Dilemma

How can educators meet the needs of all students in today's middle schools?

The Status Quo

Public school education in America at all levels is in a quandary as to how to best meet the federal and state requirements for the *No Child Left Behind (NCLB)* program, and the federal update to the *Individuals with Disabilities Act (IDEIA)*. All stakeholders of public education, from parents to school personnel, face the ever-increasing problem of how to raise student test scores while maintaining the integrity of their curriculums and the developmentally appropriateness of their instruction programs. Educators have been dealing with this issue since the release of the 1984 national study on education, *A Nation at Risk.*

Throughout the 1980s and 1990s, and continuing today, schools have become the target of school improvement programs and change processes all designed to increase the quality of education. Unfortunately, the only instrument identified to determine this improvement and program quality has been standardized test results. These test scores have become the sole criteria used to distinguish the good schools (the schools that are improving) from the bad schools (those that are not).

School and community leaders have attempted every type of program reform, from remediation, with a move back to the 3 Rs (the basics of reading, 'riting, and 'rithmetic), to acceleration (by moving upper level class content down to lower grade levels). All efforts have been focused on increasing the rigor of academic requirements without regard to the developmental appropriateness of the instruction or the social equity for students.

The penalty for not meeting the standards established for student test scores is a threatened reduction of state or federal funds or both and, in worst-case scenarios, a voucher system that allows parents to choose their children's schools. For schools that fail to make adequate progress over time, the state can take control of the school and replace the administrative and teaching personnel. School closings are rare; however, states have utilized vouchers to allow parents to enroll their children in other schools of their choice. Charter schools have been established to expand parents' choices. Reports of success achieved with voucher plans and charter schools are varied.

Students with Special Needs in Today's Schools

The requirements of NCLB and the new IDEIA focus on all children moving forward regardless of whether the child is in basic education or receiving special services through an Individual Education Plan (IEP). IDEIA requires students with special needs to be placed in the least restrictive environment, which is interpreted to mean that students with special needs whenever possible should be allowed access to the basic curriculum in regular classrooms.

The current situation in schools at all levels includes pullout or self-contained programs for special needs students. In these programs, exposure to the basic curriculum and social interaction with regular students are often limited. Pullout and self-contained classrooms often prevent students from receiving instruction in the basic education classroom. In essence, these students have little or no exposure to the regular curriculum and often times a very limited interaction with the rest of the student body. Children in these programs are segregated into classrooms that are isolated from the regular student population.

Meeting the Needs of All Students

If schools are to meet the requirements of IDEIA basic education, teachers and special education teachers must work together with a student population that is very diverse in ability and needs. Special needs students must receive basic education in regular classrooms and be guaranteed interaction with other students. At the same time, the instruction they receive must be appropriate for their needs and abilities. This places an extreme amount of pressure on teaching staff to be accommodating, yet accountable, for every student's individual goals.

The placement of more requirements on schools in general exacts a heavy toll on professional teaching and administrative staff, budgets, and school morale. Improvement is definitely needed; however, stripping the school's curriculum to the three Rs and placing higher levels of coursework at the lower grade levels is not the answer. Though it may help to some degree, an increase in school budgets won't necessarily cause student test scores to rise significantly. While funding must increase, dollars for teacher salaries and smaller class sizes are not the only factors needed for improvement to occur.

The outlook for middle level teachers, students, and parents seems even bleaker. It is the middle level of schooling that has received the most criticism from the public and from policymakers. Critics have identified grades five through nine as the weak link in education. Ever since the 1980s, American middle schools have been held responsible for everything that is wrong with education. It is the authors' contention that the real blame lies not with all middle schools, but with those that changed the name over their doors from junior high to middle school, but did little to alter what went on inside.

The-Test-Is-Everything Mentality
● ●

The *No Child Left Behind* Legislation (2002), with its focus on test scores, makes it increasingly difficult for schools to maintain a balance in their programs between academic rigor (required by NCLB) and developmental appropriateness and social equity (required by IDEIA). These three program objectives form the foundation of middle level education, according to the National Forum for Accelerating Change in Middle Level Education (2001), and support the 14 attributes of a well-rounded middle level program recommended by the National Middle School Association in its *This We Believe* publication (2003).

Schools with a junior high focus and organizational plan find it difficult, if not impossible, to focus on academic rigor, as required by the NCLB legislation, and to provide developmentally appropriate instruction for all students, including those with special needs, as required by the IDEIA. The prevailing mentality, *that the test is everything and the only thing*, leaves no leeway for developmentally appropriate instruction or equity of access to the best curriculum for all students. The belief that a test is the only measure by which to judge the quality of a school may address the component of academic rigor, but it disregards the developmental appropriateness and social equity that represent two-thirds of what a good middle school is.

Meeting IDEIA Requirements

Today's teachers and administrators must understand the *Individual Education Program (IEP)* process in order to provide a quality education, with high expectations, for children with special needs. In addition, since IDEIA requires all schools to make parents equal partners in deciding the appropriate support and services for children with disabilities, parents must also understand and participate in the IEP process.

The only school organization that meets the rigorous and extensive demands of both laws, NCLB and IDEIA, is not junior high organization, but rather a balanced middle school. The IEP process parallels the middle school philosophy of high expectations for all students at a developmentally appropriate level in a socially equitable manner.

In order for middle grade schools to meet the requirements of both NCLB and IDEIA, they must become true middle schools. These middle schools share the following common attributes:

- Brave and courageous leaders with a shared vision

- Teams of teachers who value and share high expectations for all students

- An inviting, supportive, and safe environment for all

- Grouping and regrouping of all students on a regular basis in an exclusionary environment where appropriate

- A flexible block schedule that is controlled by the teachers and based on student needs

- An adult advisory program, which provides an advocate for every student, as part of the regular schedule

- Diversified teaching methods based on brain-based research that engage students in active learning

- Parents as partners in the planning, design, and responsibility for implementation of all programs

- Community involvement in the school and its programs

10

Once the attributes are in place, the schools must provide:

- Curriculum that is appropriate, relevant, and demanding;

- Multiple learning and teaching strategies that appeal to students' diversity and individual needs;

- Assessment and evaluation programs that promote quality learning and represent high academic standards;

- Structures within the building that support building relationships and learning;

- An emphasis on health, wellness, and safety which permeates the community of learners; and

- Support and guidance services that are versatile and comprehensive.

This We Believe Publication,
National Middle School Association (2003)

This book takes the mystery out of differentiating education for middle school students with special needs. It explains a successful model for an inclusive middle school whose components and practices meet the intent and requirements of both the NCLB and the IDEIA. In addition, it provides tips on understanding, writing, and implementing an IEP so that readers can avoid the *ten most common mistakes* made in IEP writing.

The world today finds educators at a loss for implementing change and meeting the new requirements under the traditional school models. Educators' plates are full. It is important to find ways to make it possible for educators to meet these requirements.

The Educator's Dilemma

— The Parent/Advocate's View —

During my time as an advocate for children with special needs, I have witnessed many administrators and teachers fighting an uphill battle with unions, community opinion, and just plain ignorance as they explain the value of educating children with special needs within the general education curriculum. My hat goes off to these brave and courageous leaders.

Children with disabilities have so much to give—not only to schools, but also to our communities. When these children receive an appropriate education, they become independent, taxpaying adults who strengthen the economy. They become assets, rather than liabilities.

Unfortunately, not until the law began to demand that children with disabilities be included in statewide testing, did many administrators, teachers, and communities realize that children with disabilities should be held accountable for educational objectives. These children could no longer be treated as "disposables." There were consequences if they did not progress towards meeting state standards like their peers.

The middle school concept, if implemented correctly, has always been inclusive and successful in its education of special needs children. Schools all over the country should see the middle school concept as an answer to the question: "How do we teach these kids?"

— The Administrator's View —

Since 1983, the report of the National Commission on Excellence in Education, *A Nation at Risk*, has encouraged all levels of education to examine their practices more critically than ever before. American society had become increasingly concerned with students' test scores as compared to those of other countries. The fear was that the declining performance indicated a declining quality of American students. If this assumption were correct, the decline might hinder America in maintaining its leadership position in the world market of the 21st Century.

Until the 1980s, education remained a state and local issue. After the release of the *A Nation at Risk* report and the concerns it raised, education became a federal concern.

The *No Child Left Behind* legislation (NCLB), reauthorization of the *Individuals with Disabilities Education Act 1997*, and more recently the *Individuals with Disabilities Education Improvement Act of 2004*, are responsible for the continuing federal control over education. Much has been discussed and debated since 1983 about changes in education, but few have been successfully implemented.

Chapter 2

The Middle School Solution

Is the middle school model the answer for all students, including students with special needs?

The Middle School Model and Special Needs Students

NCLB and IDEIA requirements parallel middle school philosophy. All three are focused on meeting the individual needs of all students.

- The IDEIA emphasis is on meeting the special needs of all children through their access to the general education curriculum. Children with special needs not only must have access to the general education program, they now also must make progress in it.

- The NCLB focus is on having highly qualified teachers in all classrooms. Teachers must ensure that the academic content meets the needs of all children.

- Middle school philosophy is concerned with providing quality education for all students in an inclusive, developmentally appropriate environment with teachers trained in middle level teaching skills and strategies. These teachers must have high academic expectations for all students. The middle school philosophy of teacher teams and the inclusion of all students works well for special needs students in general education classes.

At no time previously in the more than 30 years of middle school existence has middle level education been faced with the current level of crisis. Today's *No Child Left Behind* legislation places the emphasis on academic rigor and the TEST as the only measurement of improvement. The task of educators to comply with the requirements of NCLB and IDEIA is difficult to meet within the current junior high model of departmental organization, period-by-period scheduling, and no common planning for teachers. The research is clear: in schools that have faithfully implemented the middle school components, student achievement has increased (Felner, 1997). The middle school model with the components of teaming, grouping and re-grouping, inclusion, common planning, and flexible schedule and advisory/advocacy, provides the vehicle to meet the requirements of both NCLB and IDEIA. Middle school leadership must take the lead in developing the programs and structures that assist young adolescents in their progression from the elementary through the middle years to the high school.

Educate the Public, Involve Parents, and Reach Out to the Community

The prevalence of negative publicity about education makes it very difficult for parents and the public to accept that the middle school model is the best one to utilize in providing for all student needs. The model is tainted with suspicion regarding test scores, quality of education, and dropout rates. Most parents and community members were educated at a different time and in a different manner than their children. Middle schools were not a reality for many of the parents of our students; or perhaps the schools they attended had "Middle School" over the door, but junior high methods inside. This lack of common experience and understanding leads to the mistrust that commonly occurs among parents, teachers, and administrators. Many parents have little faith in schools, and this level of trust has only decreased in recent years. For parents of special needs students, the mistrust intensified with the reauthorization of IDEA 1997. State test scores revealed the fact that special needs students were not receiving the basic curriculum in their self-contained and pullout classrooms.

The architectural design and arrangement of most schools adds to the diminished trust level of parents. The office areas of school buildings have been institutionalized. Their high counters separate the staff from students and parents. Principals sit behind desks, instead of at tables with parents and students. Office staff members, in many cases, are unable to understand the language and customs of the students in their buildings.

Imagine instead, a welcome room, serving freshly brewed coffee and cookies, staffed by parent volunteers who speak the languages of the non-English speakers. This room makes visitors to a school feel welcomed and cared for. Directions posted in different languages could help those who are struggling with their own language issues, as well as show respect for families' cultures.

The principal and the leadership team of administrators and teachers must reach out not only to parents, but also to the community, in order to grow the trust level and support of the school and its programs. Neighborhood coffee hours for attendance zone residents are one way to solicit parent support and participation. In high minority areas, church leaders are often a crucial group to use as a resource in the development of positive relationships. Many community organizations that provide services to families have the trust of the adults in the community, and so partnering with these organizations can give the school an entrée into their trust. If well-respected pastors and leaders of community agencies understand and speak highly of a school, they then become centers of influence for the school and its programs.

Meeting with parents and community residents on their own turf to explain how the school is helping children can also build the trust level. In other words, teachers and administrators must take their school to the community. Middle level leaders, as part of their mission and job responsibility, must educate the public so that the public can make informed decisions about what is best for their children.

Priority: Teachers Trained for the Middle Level

Often times, many of those teaching at the middle level are there because of a forced transfer. With the mobility of today's families, schools find themselves in either a growth situation where they are adding staff, or in a *rift situation* where they are losing or reassigning staff. The rift process for teachers and staff is often accomplished on a negotiated seniority basis. Because of the overlap of teacher certifications for elementary and secondary in most states (1–8 and 7–12), the middle level school becomes a convenient assignment for excess elementary and high school staff members, or for those not having success at their trained level. Regardless of how a teacher is placed, in most of these forced transfer cases, teachers who are reassigned to the middle level are unhappy about being there. This makes implementing innovative middle level components a very difficult and trying process. It definitely requires a leader who is both enthusiastic and dedicated.

Some states have created licensure for the Grade 5–9 or Grade 4–9 certifications. Universities are beginning to produce teachers who are trained for the middle level. However, since NCLB legislation with the requirement of "highly qualified" teachers, the emphasis has been placed increasingly on content knowledge and seat time. As a result, the ideal of having two planning periods— one for team planning and one for individual planning—is being replaced with one period, and teachers are teaching seven- or eight- periods each day instead of five or six periods.

Working Together for Successful Middle School Experiences

Unprepared teachers, legislatively restricted elective courses, and limited teacher planning time severely limit the possibility of a successful, developmentally appropriate middle school experience. Leadership is needed, both in the classroom as well as the district and principal's office, to prevent the loss of these essential middle level education components. If professional educators, who are the advocates for early adolescent students, don't actively promote what should be taught in classrooms and explain how the teaching and learning should be organized and delivered, who will?

The old saying, "It's easier to gain forgiveness after the fact, than permission before," is certainly worth pursuing at this juncture. Time for planning and instruction can be achieved if everyone works together. In order to achieve flexible scheduling, implement staff development strategies, and preserve the fragile educational structure called middle school, educators must be creative.

The Middle School Solution

In order to meet the needs of early adolescents, especially those with special needs, a restructuring of junior high organization and program components must occur. The emphasis must be placed on implementing middle school components correctly and eliminating the "little high school" practices and procedures that are so prevalent in many of today's so-called middle schools. What the public often fails to realize is that the middle school concept was developed precisely because junior high schools had not worked for this age group for many years. NCLB and IDEIA require schools to meet the needs of all students and to prepare them for the academic rigors of high school. Middle school organizational structure and practices best meet these requirements.

In the typical junior high model, teachers are not organized into teams nor do they have common planning with each other or the special needs teacher. In addition, they do not share the same basic education students or special needs students who are often isolated in pullout classes. Therefore, the typical junior high model ensures there will be no or very limited access to the basic education curriculum for students with special needs. This lack of access to the basic education curriculum is the major complaint of parents of special needs students in the junior high model, as well as in the improperly implemented middle school. The fully implemented middle school model with its emphasis on inclusion of all students and the practice of grouping and regrouping serves everyone. It takes brave and enthusiastic administrators and teacher leaders to bear the responsibility and support for an educational environment that is inclusive by design and provides a quality learning environment that is developmentally appropriate, socially equitable, and academically challenging so that all students (not just some) can reach their fullest potential.

Parents of special needs students have continually sought services for their children from the public schools. Schools were mandated to provide an appropriate education to students with special needs through the Federal Education for All handicapped Children Act of 1975, (94-142). Through the reauthorization of IDEA in 1997 and the 2004 IDEA Improvement Act, schools now must not only provide access in the general education curriculum, but also show evidence that students with disabilities are making progress in it. Many schools have difficulty in meeting these legal requirements because of the more popular junior high organization and practices that continue to exist in our schools. This presents a problem for both schools and parents. The middle school model has the necessary components to accommodate the needs of all students, but the components must be properly implemented.

The Middle School Solution

There are many reasons that middle school components have not been implemented properly, but I believe the following to be the leading causes:

1. It is easier to teach in a junior high structure where students are grouped by ability. The teacher in a junior high has to prepare lessons for only one ability group. Students with special needs, who often learn differently, are isolated into self-contained pullout groups. As a consequence, these students receive little or no exposure to the basic education curriculum.

2. It is easier for a teacher to lecture for an entire class period than to provide hands-on learning experiences. The lecture method is the traditional teaching style for junior and high schools. The middle school model includes a variety of teaching strategies that enhances learning for developing early adolescents. Based on research with early adolescent learners, we know that their learning is enhanced with hands-on instruction where activities allow them to move more frequently. This movement accommodates the physical changes that students are experiencing at this stage of their development.

3. Placing teachers in teaching teams is easier on paper, than it is in practice. Teaming and the associated common planning time are costly for school districts. However, the middle school concept, when properly implemented, uses teaming and common planning as a cornerstone for success. In order to serve all students, the four basic core teachers and the special education resource teacher must be available for planning at the same time. Common planning gives teachers time to improve their teaching skills to meet the diverse needs of all students.

4. Learning is much more difficult for students when experiences from class to class are not connected. Content teachers often teach in isolation without sharing what they are teaching and what students are learning in their classrooms. Therefore, students are left on their own to see the connections between the subjects they learn.

(continued)

Brain-based research has shown that the mind is a pattern-seeking organism that attempts to connect patterns as it learns (Cain and Cain). Without the collaborative effort of team teaching, early adolescent students, who characteristically have extremely short attention spans, have a difficult time making these connections. When an early adolescent also has a learning disability, making connections becomes even harder.

5. The common grouping practice at both the elementary and high school levels is to place students in groups by ability, thus creating the pullout model. Research demonstrates that this practice is not as effective for all students as the middle school model's practice of inclusion, grouping, and regrouping. Thus the pullout model, which begins in elementary and is continued in high school, makes it difficult or often impossible to implement and sustain inclusion, grouping, and regrouping at the middle level.

In traditional elementary schools, students are separated by ability for reading and math groups. The policy of not exposing special needs children to the general education curriculum begins there. At the high school level, we separate students not only by phased levels of content courses such as Algebra and Honors Algebra, but also by college prep, tech prep, and general education.

So the middle school philosophy of inclusion becomes extremely difficult to explain to teachers, parents, and the general public, who are used to grouping by ability at the other levels of schooling. Is it any wonder the middle school philosophy is such a difficult sell?

We need to remember that if we continue to do things the way we have always done them, we will get the same results. One definition for insanity is "doing the same thing, the same way, over and over again, and expecting a different outcome."

Chapter 3

Parent Involvement

How can educators assure that parents are an integral part of the student's learning team?

Research on Parent Involvement

Parents are a valuable component of students' academic and social success. Studies linking parent involvement with a variety of student cognitive and affective outcomes are extensive (Cotton & Wikelund, 1989; Desimone, 1999). Parent involvement has been linked with many different student outcomes including: increased achievement on tests, decreased dropout rates, improved attendance, improved student behavior, higher grades, greater commitment to schoolwork, and improved attitude towards school. When parents are actively involved in their children's education, their children do better in school. The academic level of the parent, their socioeconomic level, and their ethnic or racial origin are not the determining factors for academic success. The main determining factor is the attitude of the parents towards education (University of Chicago, 1999).

These results are a very important reason to want as much parent involvement as possible. Once parents are more involved in the school, they also come to understand the challenges schools face. Parents must understand the day-to-day rigor of education. Parents who get involved value and support who and what a good teacher does. Their support improves the overall morale of teachers. The more parents are involved, the more connections are made, and schools become the heart of the community—not a separate entity. When parents develop more confidence in the school system and teachers have a higher opinion of parents, they both have higher expectations for their children and their students.

Why Is Parent Involvement Lost in Middle Schools?

In this day and age parent involvement is limited. At the middle school level, early adolescents have a need to develop a sense of self and independence that is separate from their families; many of them instinctively withdraw. In response, parents back off. These changes are natural; parents should let their early adolescents make their own decisions in order for children to develop a sense of identity and responsibility for their actions. However, the distinction between being involved parents and being parents that inhibit their child's reach toward independence is a fine one—one that many parents do not know how to make. It is often much easier to distance oneself from the angst, hysteria, hormones, and drama that children this age bring to one's life. Teachers and administrators must find a way to help families with the distinction. We must find a way to keep parents involved in their children's lives—both at home and in school.

Parent Involvement In NCLB Legislation

Parental involvement always has been a centerpiece of Title I. However, for the first time in the history of the *Elementary Secondary Education Act* (ESEA), this involvement has a specific statutory definition. The statute defines parental involvement as the participation of parents in regular, two-way, and meaningful communication involving student academic learning and other school activities, ensuring that:

- Parents play an integral role in assisting their child's learning
- Parents are encouraged to be actively involved in their child's education at school
- Parents are full partners in their child's education and are included, as appropriate, in decision-making and on advisory committees to assist in the education of their child

Parental involvement provisions in section 1118 of the ESEA, Title I, Part A provide for substantive involvement at every level of the program. Parents should be included in the development and implementation of the state and local plan, and in carrying out the *Local Education Agency* (LEA) and school improvement provisions. Section 1118 contains the primary Title I, Part A requirements for the LEAs and schools related to involving parents in their children's education. It is this section that specifies parent and community participation in all aspects of the school improvement process.

Although section 1118 is extensive in scope and has many requirements for LEAs and schools, the intent is not to be burdensome. These provisions reflect good practice in engaging families in helping to educate their children, because students do better when parents are actively involved in the education process, both at home and at school. The definition of parental involvement in NCLB sets the parameters, in conjunction with other sections of the law, by which the LEA will implement programs, activities, and procedures to involve parents in Title I, Part A programs. (*Parent Involvement Title I,* Part A U.S. Department of Education, 2004)

IDEA and Parent Involvement

Parents can play a number of important roles in their relationship with their child's school. They are care providers, political advocates, and facilitators of professional decisions. Parents of children with disabilities have the added responsibility of helping plan for the education of their children. These parents must be involved in discussions about how educators can work effectively with their children and help the professional educators to create meaningful individualized education programs (IEPs).

The role as a committee member and educational decision maker in creating IEPs was established in 1975 by the *Education for All Handicapped Children Act,* now known as *Individuals with Disabilities Education Act* (IDEA). Even though parent involvement is a defining feature of IDEA, Congress, as part of the 1997 reauthorization of IDEA, believes that parental involvement needs additional emphasis. As a result, parents' rights and responsibilities are named as a necessary element in appropriate and individualized educational programming. Schools must provide an opportunity for active parental participation in all decisions about the education of children (Council for Exceptional Children, 2002).

The involvement of parents in the IEP process has many benefits:

- Increasing the teacher's understanding of the child's environment
- Adding to parents' knowledge of the child's educational setting
- Improving communication between parents and the school
- Increasing the school's understanding of the child
- Increasing the likelihood that, with improved understanding between home and school, mutually agreed upon educational goals will be attained

The Intent of Middle School Design

The middle school movement began in the late 1960s as a new design of the upper elementary and junior high schools. As societal changes were occurring in America and the country was moving away from an industrialized economy, concern was growing that junior high schools were not meeting the needs of early adolescent students. The junior high school had been designed to prepare students for high school. The junior high organization was similar to that of the traditional high school, with departmentalization and students and teachers being assigned randomly period by period throughout the day. The departmentalization and random assignment of students reinforced the practice of grouping students with special needs in separate segregated classes with a curriculum different from the basic education regular students received. In addition to being denied access to the basic education curriculum, students with disabilities were often held to lower expectations in these separate special education classes.

Junior highs were in fact a miniature version of high schools. As a scaled down high school, the junior high's organizational structure served the needs of the majority of older adolescent junior high school students, but not the needs of early adolescent students (who comprised the majority of junior high school students) or the needs of junior high students with disabilities. In addition, teachers often lacked the content expertise and expectations necessary to serve the upper elementary grades. Therefore, the early adolescent students in grade five through grade nine were essentially caught in the "middle" between elementary and high school.

In answer to this dilemma, the new middle school organization was designed. Teachers were placed on interdisciplinary teams with common planning periods. Together, the teachers were to act as advocates for the students they saw every day. Unfortunately, while the name over the school door changed to middle school, many of the traditional characteristics of junior high school remained. In addition, many uninformed parents believed that their students did not need their support. Some parents developed a blind trust in the school system. The school would always do what was right for their child.

This reaction was not true for most parents of children with special needs. These parents distrusted the middle schools; the *school clock* was ticking for their children, who had only a few years left to master basic skills before graduation.

In order to gain the participation and support of all parents whose children were in the basic program, as well as those with special needs, additional middle grade program components were designed and implemented, requiring meaningful parent participation in the education process. The middle school components of teaming, common planning, advisory, and flexible scheduling were developed to provide support for early adolescent students, and the addition of parent involvement became critical for the successful implementation of these components.

It All Sounds Good . . . So What Really Happened?

IDEA and the school improvement process of the 1990s required schools to open the door to parental involvement. Federal law and state policy now required opportunities be provided for parents to sit on school councils and be part of the improvement process. IDEA required parent involvement in the IEP process. In schools that were truly middle schools by design and program implementation, parents were afforded a meaningful opportunity on these improvement committees and in the IEP process. However, schools that simply replaced the words "Junior High" with the words "Middle School" over the door, but retained many of the traditional junior high practices, often did not provide for parental participation.

The manner in which parents are treated in a school—for example, the welcome they receive or the way their concerns are handled—creates the distrust factor that exists in many schools today. In addition, times have changed in American society.

With the negative press public education has received in the wake of the release of the national report on education, *A Nation at Risk*, and the No Child Left Behind legislation, schools no longer enjoy the prestigious position of trust evident in the early years of the last century. Barriers have been erected between the schools and the community and parents of the children they serve. In order to have parents engaged in schools, educators must remove these barriers and make school an inviting place for parents and students.

Communication Is Key

The lack of communication between home and school can add to feelings of alienation. Lack of effort from school officials, combined with the normal lack of communication that develops between many early adolescents and their parents, can leave parents in the dark as to what is happening at school. It's important to understand that as children seek their independence from their parents and adult authority, communication between parent and child occurs less frequently. Thus, parents often have no idea of what is happening in school or the life of their child. The only ones who know what is going on are the students.

The school environment provides the means for students to network daily with each other, and allows them to keep their parents in the dark. Since the parents know only what their children tell them, they are often armed with misinformation. In addition, some parents' willingness to accept their child's interpretation of what happens at school, without talking to a teacher or administrator, makes communicating with them difficult, if not impossible. In today's society, educators are experiencing a lack of respect from their students that, in many instances, is condoned by parents. The negative press schools have been receiving concerning poor student test scores and the lack of quality in education only fuels this lack of respect.

What Can Be Done to Increase Parental Involvement?

To increase parent involvement in a school, educators must first determine the community's perception of what is working and what is not working in the local schools. Establishing a parent advisory council with parents who are already involved is a good starting point. This council should have representation from all school stakeholders—teachers, administrators, parents, community leaders, and, where appropriate, students.

In developing a parent involvement program for the school, the following questions should be asked:

- Who are the parents involved in the school?
- How did these parents become involved?
- Is there a diverse representation of parents presently involved in the school?
- How do the students feel about parent involvement?
- What does each of the groups represented on the advisory committee understand parent involvement to be?

The answers to these questions can be utilized to determine the level of parent interest in the school and where the gaps are in demographic and geographic representation. A plan should then be developed to solicit parents from groups and areas not represented on the council. The goal should be to expand the parent base so that all segments of the school community are represented.

Once a representative parent group is identified, the next step is to take the school out into the community. *Taking the school into the community* involves presenting the school and its programs in the neighborhoods that comprise the attendance zones of the school, or in other words, on their own *turf*. It is crucial that educators are willing to open the school to meaningful participation of parents, and that community members are welcomed as programs are established and implemented. In an effort to gain this crucial component of parent involvement and trust in schools, educators can try many different options.

A NOTE FROM SANTO REGARDING PARENT
ATTENDANCE AT SCHOOL CONFERENCES

I often hear, "I don't have the time, "I work," and "This is your job, not mine." What we need to remember is that most school conferences are held during the workday, and not all parents are in a position to be able to leave during the workday. Unfortunately, many of our school union contracts do not provide for teachers to meet during off-hours. This becomes an impossible situation, and one for which we cannot blame parents. Their livelihood must come first. School becomes pretty unimportant if there is no food for the table. Is it any wonder that parents have lost trust and respect for our schools and educators? In dealing with all parents, we must constantly and consistently demonstrate that we genuinely care for them and their children. We must make the school a friendly, safe, and welcoming environment for students and parents.

Three Ideas Guaranteed
to Enhance Parent Participation

1. **Personal good news phone calls.**

   Teachers can take the time to make a personal phone call to let parents know their child is doing well. Many parents, particularly those with special needs students, never receive calls to tell them good news! Parents like hearing good things about their children. Make it a habit to call a family once a week with good news; it will make the first call about bad news much easier.

2. **Provide awards to all students in the school system.**

   Parents will come to school to see their children receive awards. These awards can be for any accomplishment during the grading period.

   It could be as simple as the student who is the first one in his seat for social studies in fourth period class. (Be creative and think of a way to honestly recognize every child.) *Children who are successful at any one thing will try harder at everything.*

3. **Donuts with Dad and Muffins with Mom**

   This is an excellent way to get parents into the school before school starts in the morning. Introducing their parents and greeting other parents is an excellent way to teach social skills to children. Also, parents have the opportunity to meet other parents of students who share daily classes with their children.

Beyond the Parents

Administrators and teachers have a responsibility to recruit and support parent involvement in their schools, but they cannot stop there. Schools must reach out to enlist the support of the entire community in the effort to educate children. Community agencies and churches that support families are good places to start building a team of people (beyond parents) who can assist in the development of parental involvement. Gone are the days when schools could stand alone. Opening the doors of new schools is a much easier task for school leadership teams when the school is taken out into the community.

The responsibility for creating the vision for any school falls squarely on the principal and the leadership team of the school. The leadership team must be representative of all stakeholders, including parents and the extended community.

Every member of the team has a sphere of influence and can use it to reach others. Teachers and administrators must create opportunities for interaction with parents. Parents must always feel welcomed and valued. Learn about the ethnic, cultural, and socioeconomic backgrounds of students. Make sure parents feel they are being heard. Provide as many realistic opportunities as possible for families to visit the school. Be mindful of parents' work schedules. Invite them to serve on school advisory committees and listen to their input. Sound impossible? Not really. Just start with one thing at a time. **The key is to start**.

– A NOTE FROM SANTO –
HELPFUL INSIGHTS FOR IMPLEMENTING
THE MIDDLE SCHOOL MODEL

My experience as principal and director of middle level programs has provided me the opportunity to lead the change process in three different middle school settings. Parent involvement was the cornerstone in all three of the schools as we attempted to improve school programs. Each school presented a set of different challenges; however, soliciting parent involvement was the initial starting point in the development of all three programs.

*In each situation, **taking the school to the community** was the most important aspect of building parental involvement. When parents see a school's willingness to meet on their turf instead of its own, they respond positively. The initial effort will open a host of opportunities to demonstrate the school's sincere desire to solicit parental and community involvement. Keep in mind that the goal is to fully implement the major components of a quality middle school in order to better serve all students, and that parental involvement is the key to insure success.*

Here are three experiences that may provide insight as you solicit parent involvement and implement the middle school model in your own school:

Pine Ridge Middle School

My first position as principal occurred during the 1980s at Pine Ridge Middle School in Naples, Florida. The school had an excellent reputation and was located in a middle class neighborhood. The district was in a fast growth area of the community and beginning to experience a high mobility rate. The teachers were concerned with the growing numbers of parents who were uninvolved with their child's education.

In an effort to bring the school to the neighborhoods, we planned a series of *coffee hours* during the fall semester and repeated them during the winter and spring. Their purpose was two-fold:

- First, we wanted to take the school into the community. We wanted to meet with parents and community members on their own "turf" rather than ours.

- Secondly we wanted to provide an opportunity for the neighborhoods to come together—a chance to meet each other and discuss issues and concerns that perhaps the school could assist with.

During these coffee hours, something interesting happened that highlighted the need to bring these parents together. On one particular occasion, the hostess and I were greeting parents at the front door of her home when a visiting parent expressed his pleasure in meeting her. It seemed the visiting parent had arrived in the neighborhood the previous year, and they had not yet met. As the conversation continued, I was shocked to learn they were backyard neighbors.

As modern day families focus on the need to provide for their children, they become mobile often with both parents employed to make ends meet. They work long hours away from home, and easily become less connected to their neighborhoods than they once were. The coffee hours provided parents a chance to network and find out what was happening at the school with their children, while bringing neighbors together to meet and get to know one another. In this manner, we were able to provide a structured support program for the students and the school's programs, and parents became more involved with their school and their children's education.

The information gathered at these meetings gave the school a place to start. Since all segments of the neighborhoods were invited—parents, religious and community leaders, etc.—we used the occasions to recruit individuals. We asked them to volunteer in assisting us to engage additional parents in their children's education by:

- identifying the strength of the information that was collected at each meeting, and deciding what changes needed to be made to better communicate with the community;

- outlining all school, family, and community connections that could assist both the school and the neighborhoods;

- developing a plan for parent participation from each neighborhood; and

- adjusting the plan each year to better serve the needs of the school and the neighborhoods.

Manatee Education Center

As director of middle and secondary programs for Collier County Public Schools in the 1990s, I had the opportunity to co-design the K-8 Manatee Education Center, also in Naples, Florida. The school design incorporated the best of what research identifies as effective teaching and organization elements in educating elementary through middle school students. Prior to the opening of the elementary division of the school in the fall of 1994, I was appointed as director of the center.

The school embraced several innovative organizational initiatives. These initiatives included five individual house structures with grades pre-K through 8th grade located in each house. The model contained the inclusion of special needs students and long-term teacher and student progression, meaning that teachers and students worked together for two years (an arrangement often called "looping"). The school was a "Break the Mold" school for the state of Florida because of this unique organization and instructional plan.

The population of the pre-K-8 center was approximately 2,000 students divided into five houses; each house included between 400 and 500 students. The house structure created "smallness" out of "bigness" by dividing a sizable population into smaller individual schools or houses. The pre-K through grade 3 was self-contained in each house. Grades 4 through 8 utilized teacher teams, with each team containing two, three, or four people.

The middle school division of the center opened in the fall of 1995 with a number of challenges. The population of the center was comprised of about 50 percent Hispanic, 30 percent Haitian Creole and African American, and 20 percent

Caucasian students. The center had a free and reduced lunch program that initially served 60 percent of the student population and grew to serve almost 90 percent of the students free and reduced lunches within the next five years. Our special education program served 25 percent of the student population. Language was also a large issue since more than 80 percent of our students were minorities who spoke 47 different dialects of language, mostly Hispanic, in their homes. Even though it is against the law, many of our non-English speaking students were misidentified as special needs because of their low English-proficiency skills. These factors were the deciding factors for both an inclusion and an immersion program to ensure that all of our students would receive the services they needed to succeed. The school and its inclusion and immersion programs were later nationally recognized as a Beacon of Excellence School for the U.S. Department of Education by the Educational Development Center of Boston.

Because a large number of students and parents could not speak or read English, we established a Welcome Room where students could spend up to two weeks before being paired up with another student who spoke their language. Our Welcome Room was staffed with an adult who understood and spoke their native language. Everything in the room was labeled in both English and their native language. It provided a non-threatening environment where students could "get a handle on" the English language and school culture. Once students were comfortable, they were assigned a class and teamed with their buddies to assist them in further learning the culture and language. This process demonstrated to the parents of non-English speaking students that we respected their language and heritage, and were concerned with their child's transition into the school culture.

At the same time, we contacted the ministers of the Haitian and Hispanic churches to assist us in recruiting parents for our parent-teacher groups and school improvement committees. Often we would speak at the churches on church service days and had a translator on site to assist us in explaining our programs to parents and other members of the community. Our parent meetings were held at night in either the school or church halls. Often two translators were present, and parents who spoke Spanish or Creole would pick up a headset as they entered the meeting so they were able to hear and participate in their native language.

We held parent education nights where students would demonstrate for their parents what they were learning in class. Rotary and other civic clubs were encouraged to participate in mentoring programs. A special feature of these meetings was food. Often parents wanted to share special cultural dishes and delighted in preparing and bringing food that could be shared. Our goal was to make parents feel welcomed and help them realize that the school was their school, rather than ours. Several community agencies became partners with the school in providing medical and social services to parents and families. Once parents felt welcomed and a part of the school, it was easy to solicit their support and attendance at meetings, tutoring sessions, and IEP meetings.

Grant Middle School

In the summer of 2002, I became the director of middle school programs in Marion, Ohio. The Marion City Board of Education had decided to utilize money, secured through a state competitive grant of lottery dollars, to build a new high school and three elementary schools, and to combine the three middle schools into one called Grant Middle School. The board had appointed a middle school transition team to develop a transition program plan for the school. The transition team spent two years in the development of the plan, which was based on the most recent research on middle level education. My task in Marion was to oversee the transition of the existing three middle schools into the new Grant Middle School, projected to open in the fall of 2004.

The community was steeped in tradition, with generations of Marionettes having attended the three middle schools over the past 60 years. To make things even more difficult, each middle school was viewed as representing a specific section of the city with its own cultural and support group. One was the school on the east side of town, attended by the more socially privileged. The other two each represented especially proud sections of the community, one in the rough, higher minority, older section in the center of city, and the other on the West side, or the least privileged side of town. Each building had their die-hard supporters who could not understand how the blending of the three schools could possibly be successful. The challenge was impressive and all-consuming.

The first task was to introduce the community to the transition plan approved by the board. The plan included a program built on sound middle school philosophy with a school-with-in-a-school concept of four houses. This required we combine the three faculties, staffs, and student bodies from the current schools into four houses at the new Grant Middle School. It was important that the community, teachers, and parents understand that their role was advisory—to suggest ideas and recommendations on implementation. The school administration would decide which recommendations would ultimately be implemented. In addition, teachers had to understand the important role they would play in the transition.

In order to build trust and understanding in the community and with teachers and support personnel, we needed meaningful participation in planning from all stakeholders. To accomplish this, a series of meetings and presentations was held for the community and specific civic organizations. Minority participation in all sections of the city was especially solicited. The transition team members that had researched and developed the plan for the new middle school program were selected to facilitate the community and teacher committees' meetings. The task of the committees was to gather implementation recommendations and ideas to be used in the new middle school program. Seven committees were formed, each representing a particular component generated from topics discussed in the community meetings held in the fall. Each committee formulated several recommendations for implementation concerning their component.

The recommendations were unveiled in May of 2002. The administrative teams and teacher leaders met to discuss those that could be implemented in each of the three middle schools for the 2003–2004 school year. This would provide the leadership team with the opportunity to pilot a number of the recommendations one year before the opening of the new Grant Middle School and make adjustments prior to the start of the new school year in September of 2004. A common discipline code, curriculum components, inclusion, teaming models, and learning communities were a few of the recommendation components implemented during the 2003–2004 school year.

In a change of this magnitude, community involvement is required for support. The excellent district plan was well-researched and carefully timed to prepare the community for the change. Community leaders who could either stop the plan or move it forward were identified and solicited for their involvement. As the seven committees were formed, placement of these individuals became very important. Often times in the change process, those who oppose the proposed change are excluded. These individuals then voice doubt or criticism regarding the change and the people involved in it. Having detractors involved in the process and behind the "glass" with everyone else makes it much more difficult for them to throw stones. We needed every side of all issues represented on each committee. Making sure all the committees were balanced was crucial to our success.

Parent Involvement

Having been both a parent securing special needs services for my child and a professional advocate implementing *The Individuals with Disabilities Education Act*, I know firsthand the importance of parental involvement for children with disabilities. It is common to see parents decrease their involvement in the schools when their students reach the middle school and high school levels. Most often parents of children with disabilities do the opposite. They become more involved, instead of less involved. They are racing the clock to secure and provide for their children the necessary supports and services to prepare them for adult life. Teachers and administrators frequently misunderstand this urgency; often these over-involved parents are seen as troublemakers who interfere with school policy and issues.

Our society has changed drastically over the last 20 years. Having led many training sessions for teachers, administrators, and parents, one of the questions I love to ask these attendees is, "Who would like to be a teenager in the world today?" I have yet to get a positive reply. Children today deal with so much more than we had to. In the past, the only thing we could catch from the opposite sex was *cooties*, drugs were little orange flavored pills (Bayer baby aspirin), and most of us had both our biological mother and father living under the same roof.

Today, the divorce rate in the United States is more than 50 percent. In homes where a child is born with a disability, the rate is even higher. As a result, children with disabilities live in single-parent homes more often than children without disabilities. Poverty is another high risk factor for failure in education. While some children with disabilities are poor, educators must remember that children with disabilities may come from any socio-economic background. Rich or poor, living in single-parent or two-parent families, all children deal with a lot in this day and age. Parental involvement can make or break educational success for all children, but especially for those who have disabilities.

If parental involvement is one of the main ingredients in school success for children, why are schools and teachers not working at getting more parents involved? I know what you are thinking—"I've tried." I always view this response with mixed feelings. I know there are parents who will not engage under any circumstances. But, there is a large population of parents who, if you make them feel welcomed and valued, will come forward. As the line goes in

(continued)

the movie *Field of Dreams*, "If you build it, they will come." Educators must build this bridge to parents.

Dealing with parents of children with disabilities means dealing with parents who are going through an emotional cycle. When they first discover that their child has a disability, they may ignore it and hope it will go away or grieve the loss of their perfect child. As they finally leave these emotions behind, they advance into "fix-it" mode and become intent on "fixing" their child through any possible remedy. In my case, I put my poor son through every therapy, diet, and technique available in my quest to "fix" him. I finally realized he was not broken.

When parents make this realization, as I did, they pull themselves up by their bootstraps and start a process of self-education on their child's particular disability. Parents often have only one child with special needs. Teachers usually have several students with special needs in their classes. Therefore, parents can devote more time to researching their child's needs and, because they know their child best, are able to assist teachers and be an asset to the school.

When parents bring information into the school, teachers should take the time to read it and discuss it with them. Let parents know you appreciate the time they have spent providing this information to you. Parents may go

through this cycle many times during the course of their child's education. I personally went through it every time there was a transition in my child's education. When my son was ready to go to middle school, I went along— kicking and screaming. It had taken me years to get the elementary school teachers and administrators to understand my son's needs. Now in middle school, I had to start all over again to educate the professionals about my son and to convince them to see me as an equal partner in his education. Educators working with parents of children with disabilities need to know where each parent is in the cycle. Understanding the cycle will help educators to better understand and communicate with parents.

One of the biggest misconceptions held by teachers and administrators is that they should have all the answers. Many teachers feel that a parent who tries to give them information is implying that they don't know what they are doing, or is telling them how to do their job. No one person can possibly have all the answers for every student. Parents have lived with their child and his or her disability and know a great deal about the disorder and how the disorder affects their child. Remember *Communication 101*—people need to know they have been heard. IDEA and NCLB do not expect teachers and administrators to know everything. That is why they wrote parent involvement into the law.

Parent Involvement

My experience in administering a middle school has always focused on parental involvement. My belief in having parents involved in the school in meaningful ways always guides my efforts. The successful implementation of the essential components of a good middle school philosophy depends on parents who understand and support the efforts of the school. However, as students move through the grades, parental involvement in schools is not guaranteed. After children leave the elementary schools, close monitoring of their progress by parents occurs less frequently. It appears as though parents feel that their job of close support and supervision ends with elementary school. In truth because of their developmental level, early adolescents need parent support and presence just as much if not more than they did in the primary grades.

The exceptions to this rule are the parents of special needs children. The average school principal often views these parents as problems rather than assets to the school. Often a school organizational structure is narrow in focus, designed for servicing the regular education students that comprise the majority of the school's population. It does not accommodate parents who educators assume to be overbearing because they come to school seeking opportunities to assist in their child's education. When the program design has a limited spectrum, teachers and administrators often interpret the nature of the parents' concern as parental interference.

Do not confuse this appropriate behavior with that of the truly overbearing parent whose agenda is to dictate to the school how the education process is to be conducted. Simply because they went to school, some parents believe they know as much as, if not more than, the professional educator. This inappropriate over-involvement may occur in some instances in all schools, it is most often observed in schools where parent involvement is not encouraged. Schools of this nature present a "closed door" to parents.

For additional information about the importance of parental involvement, please read about the development and success stories of three unique middle schools on pages 89–100.

Chapter 4

Middle School IEPs

What are the essential elements of an individualized education program?

It is important to recognize that an IEP is a working document, not just a piece of paper to be filed away. The IEP should be written so that anyone reading it can understand the student's present level of performance (what the child can do), where the IEP Team wants the student to be at the end of the school year (what the child will achieve during the school year), and what accommodations or modifications or both are needed to assist the student to progress in the general education curriculum.

It does not matter what IEP form is used in writing the IEP. It is not the form that makes the IEP official; rather, it is what is written into it. The law does not require a specific form; it states only what must be in the document itself. An IEP must include the following components:

- present levels of performance
- measurable annual goals
- a description of how the child's progress toward meeting the annual goals will be measured
- a list of services that are to be provided—accommodations and modifications
- the date services, accommodations and/or modifications will begin, including a schedule of their frequency, location, and duration
- the amount of time the student will participate with nondisabled children in regular classes or nonacademic activities
- a plan for informing parents of the progress toward the annual goals (at least quarterly and/or as often as progress is reported to children without disabilities).

1 Component One: Present Levels of Performance

A statement of present levels of performance is a "word picture" of what the child can do academically and functionally in the general education curriculum. To get the information to create this picture, the IEP team will need to look at the whole child. Make sure the team members look at the child in the regular education classroom, in structured situations, in unstructured situations, at home, and interacting with his peers.

There are numerous ways to collect this information. Here are a few:

- school evaluation
- private evaluation
- test scores
- work samples
- teacher observations
- parent observations
- service providers' observations & evaluations
- functional behavior assessment

Present levels of performance should be written so that everyone on the team understands what is written. Because the IEP Team is made up of professionals as well as the parents of the student, try to avoid educational jargon. Many parents are intimidated by educational terminology and reluctant to admit they do not understand it, because they do not want to appear uninformed. The IEP process was designed to ensure parent participation and responsibility in the educational progress of their child. It is imperative that they fully understand what is written if they truly are partners in this process. Most learning plan misunderstandings happen because there is not a true consensus on the present level of the student's performance.

Examples:

What to Avoid:	Parent-friendly:	More Parent-friendly:
John can read CVC words independently.	John can read consonant-vowel-consonant words independently.	John can read consonant vowel consonant words (cat, rat, sat, mat) independently.
A parent might not understand what CVC words are.	*Some parents will struggle with this present level.*	*Stay away from subjective terminology; be specific.*

What to Avoid:	Subjective Present Level:	Specific Present Level:
John is very disruptive in class.	John is disrespectful of adult authority.	When John is placed in a situation where he is embarrassed, he will become angry and use foul language.
One team member may think tapping a pencil is disruptive; someone else may not.	*State specifically what the student can or cannot do.*	*State specifically what the student can or cannot do.*

The present levels of performance component should also address how the student's disability affects the student's involvement and progress in the general education curriculum. Ask and answer these questions as an IEP team.

- Does the student need accommodations in the general education classroom to progress in the general education curriculum?
- Does the student need modifications in the general education classroom to progress in the general education curriculum?
- Does the student's disability affect his involvement in the general education curriculum? If so, how?

Examples:

> John can progress in the general education curriculum with accommodations in the regular education classroom.
>
> or
>
> John can progress in the general education curriculum at his functioning level with appropriate modifications and supports.

Don't make the mistake of being too wordy, or a "Pollyanna." IEP Team members should be concerned only with what the student can and cannot do, not with how cute they are.

> John is a handsome young man who is a pleasure to have in class. Even though he struggles in his academics, he participates and always makes an effort to answer questions when asked. He is always polite to his peers and tries to fit in.

Although this is very nice, it does not address what the IEP team needs to understand to develop an IEP goal for the school year.

> When writing, John can use punctuation, including question marks, exclamation points, and periods. He uses capitalization for the first word in a sentence, names, and the pronoun *I*. He also understands and uses nouns, verbs, and adjectives (descriptive words).

This is a better example of what an IEP Team must know to develop a goal.

If there is not a clear present level of performance, the IEP process becomes stalled. You cannot project where a student is going if you do not know where he is performing today. Present levels of performance should always be specific, rather than broad and general. If the student moves to another school district or even out of the state, another educator should be able to pick up the IEP and know what the student can or cannot do.

Questions to ask about the present levels of performance:

1. Have present levels responses addressed both academic and functional performance?
2. Are present levels in these areas specific?
3. Are present levels understandable to everyone on the team?
4. Do the responses state how the disability affects the student's progress in the general education curriculum?

When the IEP Team can answer the above questions, they are ready to move on to component two.

2 Component Two: Measurable Annual Goals

When the reauthorization of IDEIA in 2004 eliminated short-term objectives and benchmarks, even more emphasis was placed on the writing of annual goals to measure student progress. Many IEPs had been written using short-term objectives and benchmarks as a way of measuring progress for an annual goal. It is imperative to know if the student is progressing throughout the year. The team does not want to get to the end of the school year and find the child is nowhere near his or her annual goal. Even though progress reports are sent out regularly, it is not an easy task to address progress if you have nothing to measure it by.

When the IEP Team looks at writing a measurable annual goal, they should first look at the present level of performance and ask the following questions:

- What can the student do presently in the area of the proposed goal?
- What are the general education curriculum standards in this area?
- Where is the student performing in regard to the general education curriculum?
- How much anticipated progress toward the goal will the student achieve in one school year?

When writing a goal, everyone on the team must be in agreement as to the projected progress. Parents must be able to understand the goal and how their student's progress will be measured. This is vital in making sure communication is established with the school and parents. If everyone understands the goal and everyone is in agreement as to how it will be measured, the whole team is then responsible for making sure the student is progressing toward the goal. All IEP team members, including the parents, assume responsibility for seeing that the student is progressing. Under IDEIA, it is just as much the parents' job as it is the school district's job to monitor progress.

When reference is made to state standards, the team is projecting how the child is progressing within the general education curriculum.

– A NOTE FROM DENA –

Many Special Education Educators have been instructed not to use state standards. My question to them is always "Why not?" IDEIA does not say you can't use the state standards, and isn't that what all children are tested on under NCLB? I also think that it helps the team identify where the child is performing, and can help the team measure progress. The reason NCLB pressed states to come up with state standards was to have a way to measure progress and to keep everyone on the same page. I am a firm believer in utilizing what resources we have and, in my opinion, not using the state standards defeats the purpose of having children with disabilities exposed to the general education curriculum.

When writing goals from the state standards, take time to understand their structure and format. Some terms that will be helpful to understand are:

- **Academic Content Standards**

    — Academic content standards represent what all students should know and be able to do.

    — These are overarching goals and themes.

- **Benchmarks**

    — Benchmarks are key checkpoints that mark progress toward the academic content standards.

    — Benchmarks are grouped in grade-level cluster/bands.

    — Grade-level bands will vary across content areas and should align with achievement tests where applicable.

- **Grade-level Indicators**

    — Grade-level indicators represent what all students should know and be able to do at each grade level.

    — They are checkpoints that monitor progress toward the benchmarks.

    — Grade-level indicators align with diagnostic tests.

When writing measurable goals, look at grade-level indicators, then look at the student's present level of performance to see where the student is performing.

A Specific Example of the Process

Here is a statement of John's present level of performance:

John is a young man with a learning disability.
He is in the seventh grade.

- John can write a simple sentence with capitalization and punctuation.
- John has met the state standard for a beginning second grade writing level in the area of Grammar Usage. He can use punctuation, including question marks, exclamation points, and periods. He uses capital letters for the first word in a sentence, names, and the pronoun I. He also understands and uses nouns, verbs, and adjectives (descriptive words).

1. <u>ASK</u>: What are the state standards for writing for a student in the seventh grade?

Grade Level Seven Grammar Usage

- Student uses commas, end marks, apostrophes, and quotation marks correctly. Student also knows and understands how to use semicolons, hyphens, dashes, and brackets correctly.

- Student uses correct capitalization in all areas of writing.

- Student uses all eight parts of speech: nouns, pronouns, verbs, adverbs, adjectives, conjunctions, prepositions, and interjections.

- Student uses verbs, including perfect tenses, transitive and intransitive verbs, and linking verbs.

- Student uses nominative, objective, possessive, indefinite, and relative pronouns.

- Student demonstrates proper subject-verb agreement when using collective nouns, indefinite pronouns, compound subjects, and prepositional phrases.

2. <u>THINK ABOUT</u>: At what level is John performing compared to his peers?

John is performing at least five years behind his peers.

Think: It is not realistic to expect John to perform on grade level at the end of one year.

Look at where he presently is and project how much he can realistically learn in one school year.

3. <u>LOOK AHEAD</u>: What will John be able to achieve this school year?

Since John currently meets the state standard for the beginning of second grade, the team might project that John will achieve one year of progress to the beginning of third-grade writing levels in the area of Grammar Usage. This prediction should be reflected in the student's annual goal.

4. *NOW WRITE a measurable annual goal for John.*

Since John currently meets the state standard for the beginning of second grade, the team might project that John will achieve one year of progress to the beginning of third-grade writing levels in the area of Grammar Usage. This prediction should be reflected in the student's annual goal.

Goal: John will write sentences using correct end punctuation marks, correct capitalization, with correct nouns, and verbs that are in agreement. He will understand how to write subjects and verbs that are in agreement, irregular plural nouns, possessive nouns, and pronouns that are in agreement. He will understand past, present, and future verb tenses, and use conjunctions correctly.

OR

Goal: John will write a paragraph with a topic sentence, three supporting sentences, and a closing statement showing correct grammar usage at a third-grade level.

Note: Both of these goals meet the criteria under the law as a measurable goal, but would everyone on the IEP Team better understand goal one or goal two? If the IEP team chooses to use state standards, remember that not all parents will understand the standards' terminology. However, they will be able to understand that their child is currently writing on a second-grade level and that the IEP Team is projecting that the child will progress to the third-grade level in one year.

Writing Behavior Goals

Although there are presently no state standards for student behavior, there are standards in English Language Arts in the area of Communication: Oral and Visual. Since behavior is a form of communication, use the communication standards to help write student behavior goals.

Follow these steps to write measurable annual goals for behavior.

1. Look at the grade-level indicators for a second-grade student:

> Grade Level Two
>
> *Listening and Viewing*
>
> - Use active listening strategies, such as making eye contact and asking for clarification and explanation.
> - Compare what is heard with prior knowledge and experience.
> - Identify the main idea of oral presentations and visual media.
> - Follow two- and three-step oral directions.
> - Demonstrate an understanding of the rules of the English language.
> - Select language appropriate to purpose and use clear diction and tone.
>
> *Speaking Skills and Strategies*
>
> - Demonstrate an understanding of the rules of the English language.
> - Select language appropriate to purpose and use clear diction and tone.

2. Ask: What does John presently do that is inappropriate in the classroom?

> John hands in his homework only three out of five days a week, even with verbal prompts.

How do his peers perform in this same area of behavior?

> Seventh-grade students are able complete and hand in their homework five out of five days a week without prompts.

What will John be able to do by the end of the school year?

> Goal: With verbal prompts, John will do his homework and hand it in five out of five days a week.

AUTHORS' NOTE ABOUT BEHAVIOR GOALS

IDEIA *states that anytime a behavior interferes with a student's learning or the learning of others it should be addressed on the* IEP. *If a student is identified under IDEIA with a mental health disorder, the Diagnostic and Statistical Manual on Mental Disorders (DSM-IV) is a good resource to use. The DSM-IV lists behaviors that are symptoms of mental health disabilities. This manual can be found at a Public Library.*

Disabilities such as: Oppositional Defiant Disorder (ODD), Attention Deficient Disorder with or without Hyperactivity (AD/HD), Obsessive Compulsive Disorder (OCD), and Conduct Disorder (CD) are a few of the disabilities that have behaviors that may interfere with a student's learning. When the student's behaviors are symptoms of the disability and the behaviors are interfering with the student's learning or the learning of others, there should be behavior goals on the IEP *to address the behaviors.*

If you have students that develop behaviors that are not symptoms of their disabilities, but are interfering with their learning or the learning of others, there should be a Behavior Plan developed and added as an addendum to the IEP. *The main thing to remember is that if a student is exhibiting a behavior that interferes with learning, it should be addressed. The worst thing an IEP team can do is to ignore a behavior and do nothing.*

---

3 Component Three: A Description of the Child's Progress and How it Will be Reported

Once the measurable annual goals have been written, there must be a description of how the child's progress toward meeting the annual goals will be measured and when periodic reports on the progress toward the goals will be provided to the parents. These reports should go out at least quarterly or more often depending on how often the school district reports progress to parents of children without disabilities.

Examples:

Goal:	John will write a paragraph with a topic sentence, three supporting sentences, and a closing statement. The paragraph will contain correct grammar usage at a third-grade level.
Description:	John's progress will be measured through work samples and testing. A report will be sent home quarterly to address his progress.

Goal:	John will hand in his homework five out of five days a week with verbal prompts.
Description:	John's progress will be measured through charting and observations. A report will be sent home quarterly to monitor his progress.

4 Component Four: Accommodations and Modifications — a List of Necessary Services

It is very important to know the difference between an accommodation and a modification. There is a major difference between the two, and they should not be used interchangeably.

- An ***accommodation*** is the HOW of the curriculum. An accommodation explains how the educator is going to get the information *to* the student and how the knowledge will be assessed. Some examples of accommodations are extended time, reader, scribe, and small-group instruction.

  The Special Education Teacher (Intervention Specialist) will have an expertise in this area. He or she works daily with students and is an expert in assisting how they learn.

- A ***modification*** is the WHAT of the curriculum. A modification addresses what part of the general curriculum the student needs to know to reach his or her full potential.

Examples:

A class may be required to learn all 50 states and capitals.
Modification: The student with a disability may be required to learn only the state and capital in the state of his or her residence.

Students in a science class must learn the parts of a plant and how it grows.
Modification: The student with a disability must learn how to plant, water, and make light available to vegetables.

The Regular Education Teacher has the expertise in the general education curriculum. He or she will know why students are being taught a certain concept.

It is important to remember that the IEP must include a statement of any individual appropriate accommodation that is necessary to measure the academic achievement and functional performance of the child on state- and district-wide assessments, a statement of why the child cannot participate in the regular assessment, and any particular alternate assessment selected as appropriate for the child.

Under NCLB and IDEIA 2004, most children with disabilities will participate in statewide testing to measure adequate yearly progress. All students with disabilities are to be exposed to the general education curriculum and must make progress in it. The area of appropriate accommodations and modifications is absolutely essential in determining successful outcomes. If a child is not receiving accommodations in the regular education classroom, teachers cannot give accommodations on the statewide test.

Examples:

> If John takes his regular curriculum tests in the regular education classroom and he does not need extra time, then John cannot receive the statewide testing in a small group with extended time.

But:

> If John uses a spell checker in the regular classroom he can use a spellchecker on the statewide testing.
>
> So John's list of accommodations would include: John will use a spell checker when he takes the statewide writing test.
>
> In this case, the writing test is not testing spelling; it is testing John's mastery of writing structure and fluency. Using a spellchecker is not changing the content of the test.
>
> As long as the teacher is not changing the content of the test, the same accommodations provided in the regular classroom can be provided during state testing.

5 Component Five: The Dates that Services, Accommodations or Modifications or both will begin, including a Schedule of their Frequency, Location, and Duration

When a student receives such services as occupational therapy, physical therapy, speech therapy, adapted physical education, and sensory integration, all have to be addressed on the IEP. For each support service, the IEP will include:

- the type of service
- how much service will be provided
- who will provide the service
- where that service will be given

Keep in mind that one of the most common mistakes school systems make occurs in writing this component of the IEP.

- Make sure everyone on the team understands who will be providing the service. Ask and answer questions such as, "Will the speech therapist be providing the service, or will the therapist just advise the regular education teacher?"

- Make sure to address any lag in the time between the start of school and the start of therapies. If the speech teacher doesn't start working with the students until two weeks after school starts, don't state that services will begin at the start of the school year. Put the actual start date on the IEP. Doing this will let everyone know exactly when the services are to begin.

- Be specific about how much of each service will be provided. Don't make vague statements such as "two to four times a week." Parents may assume their child is getting special help four times a week for extended time periods when the child is actually receiving service for 20 minutes, twice a week. The parents will feel they were misled, and they will begin to lose faith in the IEP team.

- Make it very clear where the services will be delivered: small group, one on one, or in the regular classroom. Most parents don't understand that many therapies can be delivered in the regular classroom.

There could be a misunderstanding if services are written this way on the IEP:

Service	Who will provide?	When will the service start?	How much time will be provided?	Where will the child receive the service?
Speech Therapy	Teacher	Beginning of the year	2 to 3 times a week for 20 to 30 minutes	In the classroom

There can be no misunderstanding if services are written this way:

Service	Who will provide?	When will the service start?	How much time will be provided?	Where will the child receive the service?
Speech Therapy	Speech Therapist	2006–2007 School Year or August 28, 2006	20 minutes, 2 times a week	Small Group in Resource Room

6 Component Six: The Amount of Time the Student will participate with Peers Without Disabilities in Regular Classes or Nonacademic Activities

Once the IEP Team has determined the services a student will require, they must then decide if the child will receive these services and modifications in the regular classroom. It is the responsibility of the IEP Team to consider first the Least Restrictive Environment (LRE). The least restrictive environment is in a regular classroom with services and supports to assist the student in achieving progress within the general education curriculum.

The IEP Team should always look at the regular classroom first, because it is there the student will get the most access to the general educational curriculum. When a student with a disability is pulled out of a regular classroom, access to the general education curriculum is limited, and academic time is lost because the student is moving from one classroom to another.

When it is necessary to pull a student out of the regular education classroom, the IEP must document how much time is being spent with children without disabilities. This information can be included in the present levels of performance and measurable annual goals.

Examples:

> With services and supports, John will be able to progress in the general education curriculum in the regular education classroom 100 percent of the school day.

> Because of the severity of John's disability, to progress in the general education curriculum he will need modifications in a small-group setting such as the resource room for 90 percent of the school day. He will participate in music and art within the regular classroom.

Chapter 5

Avoiding Mistakes

How can educators avoid the ten most common mistakes made in middle school IEPs?

Educators, Take Note!

The new procedural safeguards for writing IEPs were designed to prevent mistakes by providing a road map. Often teachers and administrators, faced with new procedures and regulations, believe that the requirements can be ignored, only to find out that the law is now very specific. There are now specific procedures for dealing with any difference of opinion between the school and parent.

The middle school philosophy is founded on a collaborative approach; parents are involved with the design and process of education. The old theory that the school should dictate what will happen to students is obsolete. Students, where appropriate, are also provided a voice in how the learning process is organized. They help to determine not only what they will learn, but also the manner in which they will learn. The middle school philosophy, when properly implemented, will reduce the occurence of the following mistakes.

The ten mistakes most commonly made while writing an IEP are:

1. All stakeholders are not at the IEP meeting.

2. Parents do not see themselves as a vital part of the IEP team.

3. Regular, ongoing communication with parents in regard to their child's education is limited or missing.

4. The IEP team is unable to articulate the present levels of performance in regard to academics, functional performance, and how the student's disability affects progress in the general education curriculum

5. The IEP team fails to address a behavior that interferes with the student's learning.

6. Goals developed are not measurable.

7. The team does not receive progress reports on IEP goals.

8. The IEP lacks specific guidelines addressing whether special services are to be provided, when services are to start, how often a student receives services, and who is to provide the service.

9. Modifications and/or accommodations are not clearly stated on the IEP.

10. Prior written notice is not provided to a parent when there is a disagreement on identification, placement, or the provision of a Free and Appropriate Public Education (FAPE)

Read the analysis of each mistake below. Think about how the mistakes can be prevented during the IEP process.

 **Mistake 1** **All stakeholders are not at the IEP meeting.**

IDEIA and NCLB are both very clear about the importance of parents being active and responsible partners in their child's education. IDEIA goes even further by mandating by law that parents are part of the decision-making process in all aspects of their child's education. The term "IEP Team" means a group of individuals composed of:

1. The parents of a child with a disability
The definition of parent is: a natural, adoptive, or foster parent of a child (unless a foster parent is prohibited by state law from serving as a parent); a guardian (but not the state if the child is a ward of the state); an individual acting in the place of a natural or adoptive parent (including grandparent, stepparent, or other relative) with whom the child lives, or an individual who is legally responsible for the child's welfare; or a surrogate parent appointed by the superintendent of the home school district.

2. Not less than **one of the child's regular education teachers** (if the child is, or may be, participating in the regular education environment)

3. Not less than **one special education teacher or special education provider**
This flexibility in the law was written to assist IEP Teams in providing appropriate participants the ability to have active participation in the development of the IEP without causing conflicts in schedules. The law also states that the IEP meeting should be at a convenient time and place for the parents. This flexibility must not be misused—the law does not provide this flexibility for exclusion of participants. Remember, excusal must be a written agreement between the local district and the parent. (For further notes on flexibility see page 59.)

There should be at least one special education provider to participate in the IEP process. When service providers such as occupational therapists, speech therapists, physical therapists, and sensory integration specialists are providing services to a student, they should have active input into the IEP process, either in physical or written form.

4. **A representative of the local education agency (LEA)** who

   • is qualified to provide, or supervise the provision of, specially designed instruction to meet the unique needs of children with disabilities;

   • is knowledgeable about the general education curriculum;

   • is knowledgeable about the availability of resources of the local educational agency.

An LEA representative does not have to be the special educational director, principal, or superintendent. The law states that anyone can be a representative, as long as they meet the requirements above. Having an LEA representative in attendance prevents having to interrupt the IEP meeting to ask someone not in attendance what services are available.

5. **An individual who can interpret the instruction implication of results of an evaluation**
When the school district initiates an evaluation for a child with a disability, they are required to have a person at the IEP meeting to interpret the evaluation results. (Most school districts will have the school psychologist attend the

meeting to explain their initial evaluation findings and how the results reflect the instruction in the classroom.) Due to the shortages and caseloads of school psychologists, the law does not state that the person interpreting the evaluation has to be a psychologist; but the person should be able to answer questions asked by the team members. Most importantly, this person must be able to explain evaluation results so that all team members fully understand the impact of the child's disability in the regular education classroom.

6. At the discretion and cost of the parent or the agency, **other individuals who have knowledge or special expertise regarding the child**, including related services personnel as appropriate
Many times there is a need to include outside professionals who bring an abundance of knowledge in the area of the child's disability. The school district, as well as the parent, can invite individuals who will assist in the development of the IEP through their experience and expertise.

7. Whenever appropriate, **the child**
It is very important for both the professionals and parents to understand the importance of children being part of their own IEP process. Young adults need to understand their disabilities and learn how to self-advocate. They are the key to their own success in the real world. Having them be part of this process is a good transition as they proceed to their post-secondary options.

> NOTE: During the reauthorization process in 2004 of IDEA H.R. 1350 passed by Congress on November 19, 2004, flexibility was written into the law. Understanding how hard it is to get schedules together to have an IEP meeting, the following provisions were added:
>
> • <u>Attendance Not Necessary</u>—A member of the IEP Team shall not be required to attend an IEP meeting, in whole or in part, if the parent of a child with a disability and the local education agency agree that the attendance of such member is not necessary because the member's area of the curriculum or related services is not being modified or discussed in the meeting.
>
> • <u>Excusal</u>—A member of the IEP Team may be excused from attending an IEP meeting, in whole or in part, when the meeting involves a modification to or discussion of the member's area of the curriculum or related services if:

1. the parent and the local educational agency consent to the excusal;
2. the member submits, in writing, recommendations to the IEP Team prior to the meeting.

- <u>Written Agreement and Consent Required</u>—A parent's agreement and consent shall be in writing.

 **Mistake 2** **Parents do not see themselves as a vital part of the IEP Team.**

Mistake 3 **Regular, ongoing communication with parents in regard to their child's education is limited or missing.**

The law states there must be parent participation in the IEP process. This is very important if parents are to take an active role in their child's education. Under IDEIA and NCLB, there is a push for more parent participation and parent responsibility in education. Gone is the day when parents dropped their children at the door and said, "Here they are. Educate them." If we are to have children achieve their full potential, it takes both parents and educators working together as a team.

During the writing of an IEP, the use of educational jargon can intimidate and alienate parents.

Example:

> We will refer the child for an IAT to see if we need to do an MFE. Then if we need to do the MFE, we will find out if he is AD/HD, LD, or SED. The results of the MFE will tell us if he qualifies for an IEP, but if he doesn't, we might be able to do a 504.

Professionals use acronyms as part of their daily language and can forget that new and undefined acronyms overwhelm parents. When working with parents, it is vital to have them fully understand what is being stated. Not only is this polite (as well as common sense), it is the law. The law states that all information given to a parent has to be understandable to them. Most misunderstandings occur when one party doesn't understand everything that is said. Avoid educational jargon.

Many times parents think they have little or nothing to add to the IEP process. They believe that the teacher is the expert and they have nothing to give. However, parents live with their child's disability everyday. They know what works and what doesn't work. Most importantly, the best way to have parents share responsibility for their child's education is to make them contributing partners in the process. There is much more to education than the five to six hours a day the child is in school. Homework, parent interaction, and the parent's attitude towards school are very important. The parent is the only person who can be responsible for this part of the child's learning.

IDEIA reinforces parent involvement by stating that parents will be equal partners both in participation and responsibility. The law is very clear. Parents have a responsibility in their child's educational success. By requiring parents to participate in the IEP process, they become responsible partners. When parents take ownership and see themselves as part of the process, there is a better chance for communication when problems arise.

Keep in mind there also needs to be communication when things are going well. Parents like to get good messages from the school, too. Parents, as well, need to communicate when they are satisfied with what is happening at the school. Educators and parents must support each other in the difficult process of raising and educating young adolescents.

– A Note from Dena –

I cannot stress enough the need for communication between the school and parents. Parents must feel comfortable enough to let the school know when something is going on at home that might affect the educational performance of their child. An educator has to feel comfortable enough to let the parent know when things are not going well at school, without worrying about the parent pointing fingers and blaming. For parents to take responsibility and an active role in their child's education, they must have a grasp on what is going on at school and assist the team in developing solutions.

Mistake 4

The IEP team is unable to articulate the present levels of performance in regard to academics, functional performance, and how the student's disability affects progress in the general education curriculum

Mistake 5

The IEP team fails to address a behavior that interferes with the student's learning

When you look at all the components of an IEP, the present levels of performance is the most important. A present levels of performance statement gives the IEP team a starting point to begin the IEP process. When the team knows exactly where the child is performing, then members can project where he or she will be by the end of the school year. If the team doesn't have an accurate present level of performance, there will be no starting point. Without a starting point, the team can't tell if a child is progressing in the general education curriculum or not.

Collect information on a student's present levels of performance from current evaluation data, work samples, tests, teachers, and parents. A present level of performance should describe what the student can and cannot do in the regular education classroom.

- How does the student perform in math, reading, and behavior in relationship to his or her peers?

- Is there an area that the child excels in, such as art, music, or sports?

Present levels of performance should give the team a good idea of how the student learns, and what supports and services are needed for the student to be successful in the general education curriculum.

A program built on strong middle school theory will provide teachers the opportunity to determine a student's accurate level of performance. Through the instructional delivery design, which allows for the grouping and regrouping of students and the use of short-term assessment, a student's progress will be continually monitored. The premise of including all students in the grouping and regrouping process allows for the inclusion of students with special needs. These students can receive services in the general education curriculum. Since the special needs teacher is included on the core academic team, and has common planning with the team, modification and accommodations can be suggested and utilized by the academic teachers. This provides the student with the opportunity to progress in the general education curriculum. Teachers and parents will be able to easily access the current ongoing level of student performance.

The statement of student's present levels of performance must be agreed upon before the IEP team can do any kind of Individual Education Program. During the IEP process, it is very important there is no misunderstanding on the present level of performance of the student.

– A NOTE FROM DENA –

Parents must understand what is being said and written in present levels of performance. Always be mindful of the parent's level of understanding. Avoid using special education jargon. Use common language a parent can understand. When you are talking about a child's present level of performance in an IEP, make sure the parent agrees. Any misunderstanding sets up a level of mistrust and can be very destructive to communication and the IEP process. Be very clear in what the present level of performance is and make certain the parent can comprehend what is being stated and written on the IEP.

Examples of ways to write for parent understanding:

Not Parent Friendly	Parent Friendly #1	Parent Friendly #2
The child can state CVC words.	The child can recognize simple consonant–vowel–consonant words such as cat, dog, rat.	John can recognize such words as cat, rat, sat, and mat.
John writes at a second grade level.	John can write a simple sentence with correct capitalization and punctuation.	John can write a sentence such as: I have a dog.
John is disorganized.	John can get his homework in 2 out of 5 days a week.	John turns in homework M T W Th F X X
John can add and subtract simple math problems.	John adds and subtracts one- and two-digit numbers. He does not understand carrying and borrowing.	John understands $\begin{array}{r}2\\+\,3\\\hline\end{array}$ $\begin{array}{r}44\\-\,22\\\hline\end{array}$

Once you have addressed the present levels of performance in the area of academics, you need to evaluate how the student is doing in the area of behavior. Anytime a behavior interferes with the learning of the student or the learning of others, it needs to be addressed on the IEP in present level of performance.

Properly implemented teaming processes, with common planning, allow teacher teams the opportunity to examine student behavior on an ongoing basis. Since the special needs teacher is part of the team, he or she has the opportunity to observe the student's behavior in different classrooms. During team planning, the special needs teacher can share strategies that worked for other teachers in dealing with the student's inappropriate behaviors.

The law states that whenever a behavior interferes with the learning of the student or the learning of others, it must be addressed on the IEP. When the behavior is a manifestation of the student's disability, there should be goals on the IEP to address these behaviors if they are interfering with the student's learning. Imagine a student with AD/HD who has a learning disability. The demonstrated behavior is being disorganized. For example, the student does not bring materials to class, hand in homework, or take home books. This behavior interferes with the student's learning. Therefore, specific goals pertaining to the student's disability of being disorganized must be included in the IEP.

Remember:

- **When writing present levels of performance statements, do not be broad and general.**

General	Specific
John comes to class unprepared.	John comes to class with classroom materials (books, pencils, and gym clothes) 2 out of 5 days a week.
John does not do homework assignments.	John hands in his homework two days out of five days a week. This increases to four out of five days if he is prompted by the teacher.

Children who have trouble focusing will receive disciplinary action for not paying attention, leaving their seat, bothering others, and being disruptive. IEP members must remember that when they are writing a present levels of performance statement in the area of behavior, the statement must be specific.

- **State exactly what the child does:**

General	Specific
John is disruptive in class.	John can focus for five minutes without being redirected. He can sit in his seat for a maximum of ten minutes without tapping his foot or pencil on the desk.
John cannot keep his hands to himself.	On four out of five days, when John is at table with his peers, he will push and punch the person next to him.

After addressing the academic, behavior, and functional performance of the student, address how the disability will affect progress in the general education curriculum:

John can progress in the general educational curriculum with accommodations and supports in the regular education classroom. John comes to class unprepared.

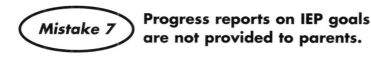

Mistake 6 — **Goals developed are not measurable.**

After the present levels of performance statements are written, writing a measurable goal is really very simple. Just look at the present level of performance and ask, "Where does the IEP team feel this student will be by the end of the school year?" Remember to write the answer to the question so that it is measurable and understandable to the parent.

Many teachers are reluctant to write measurable goals because they fear the student may not attain the goals. Each goal is meant to be an estimate of the capability of the student from the current information. IDEIA 2004 eliminated benchmarks and short-term objectives as components of the IEP process. So, the importance of writing measurable IEP goals is crucial if parents are to be well informed about their child's progress throughout the school year.

Once again the middle school teaming process, properly implemented with common planning, will assist the team in writing appropriate measurable goals. A team of teachers who have the same students assigned to them will be able to develop realistic, measurable goals. Including the special needs teacher in the team enhances this process. If the special needs teacher does not have common planning time, then the opportunity to share strategies and modifications for students with the team is severely limited.

Mistake 7 — **Progress reports on IEP goals are not provided to parents.**

Since IDEIA 2004 eliminated short-term objectives and benchmarks, it is absolutely vital that progress reports go home throughout the year, documenting for parents the student's progress toward annual goals.

During the reauthorization of IDEA in 1997, school districts were required to provide progress reports on annual goals whenever progress reports were sent home for students without disabilities. Many schools send interim reports home in the middle of the semester to let parents know how their children are progressing. If interim reports went home to all regular education students, then a progress report on the IEP goals would have been required for the students with special needs. When the district sends grade cards home, progress reports are required on the IEP goals. These measures are an effort to keep parents informed and active partners in the education of their children.

By adding a simple column on the interim and report card that speaks to the child's performance as being "at grade level," "above grade level," or "below grade level," parents are also informed that the child has met the standards at grade level or at the accommodated or modified level as specified on the IEP.

Mistake 8

The IEP lacks specific guidelines addressing whether special services are to be provided, when services are to start, how often a student receives services, and who is to provide the service.

Many school districts make the mistake of writing services on the IEP and not delivering them as they are written. Occupational, physical, and speech therapy services and small-group support are most commonly written incorrectly. The IEP will state, for example, that the student will receive physical therapy two times a week for 20 minutes and that the services will start at the beginning of the school year. The parent understands this to mean the first week of school. However, many therapists do not deliver services at the beginning of the school year. It may take them up to a month to get their schedule up and going. So the therapy does not start the first week of school, the child is not progressing, and parent trust becomes a factor.

In addition, the small-group support sessions may be part of a pullout program, which excludes or limits the child's ability to progress in the regular curriculum. The parent is often not aware that the small-group instruction service comes at the expense of the child's participation in the general education program. When the parent finds out that the student is being excluded from the general program, or exploratory program, parent trust again becomes a factor.

These problems are part of a master-scheduling problem. The law is specific. The IEP must specify the amount and length of time special modifications and accommodations will be provided. An IEP must state how the services will be delivered, who will be doing the services, and where those services will be delivered. This attention to detail will prevent misunderstandings and guarantee the best services for the student.

Example:

Starting Date: June 15th 200__

Therapy	How Often	Who	Where
Speech	2/week x 20 min	Speech Therapy	Small Group
Small-Group Instruction	3/week x 42 min	Intervention Specialist	Resource Room

The master schedule of a true middle school must accommodate a balanced program for all students. In order for that to occur, extra periods or blocks of time must be added to the day. Those students that are accelerated and those that need small-group time for either special needs or remedial work have to be accommodated without being excluded from general and exploratory programs.

An example of a master schedule that accommodates and meets these specifications is the Flexible Block Schedule.

Grant Middle School
Flexible Block Schedule

6th Grade		7th Grade		8th Grade		Exploratory Arts (E.A.)	
8:10–8:45 (35)	Activity	8:10–8:45	Activity	8:10–8:45	Activity	8:10–8:45	Activity
8:45–9:27 (42)	Core 1	8:45–9:27	Core 1	8:45–9:27	E. A. (Team)	8:45–9:27	8
9:27–10:09 (42)	Core 2	9:27–10:09	Core 2	9:27–10:09	E. A. (Prep)	9:27–10:09	8
10:09–10:50 (41)	**Flex**	10:09–10:51	Core 3	10:09–10:51	Core 1	10:09–10:50	Team
10:50–11:20 (30)	**Lunch**	**10:51–11:32 (41)**	**Flex**	10:51–11:33	Core 2	10:50–11:20	Lunch
11:20–12:02 (42)	Core 3	**11:32–12:02 (30)**	**Lunch**	**11:33–12:14 (41)**	**Flex**	11:20–12:02	Prep
12:02–12:44 (42)	Core 4	12:02–12:44	E. A. (Team)	**12:14–12:44 (30)**	**Lunch**	12:02–12:44	7
12:44–1:26 (42)	**Core 5**	12:44–1:26	E. A. (Prep)	12:44–1:26	Core 3	12:44–1:26	7
1:26–2:08 (42)	E. A. (Team)	1:26–2:08	Core 4	1:26–2:08	Core 4	1:26–2:08	6
2:08–2:50 (42)	E. A. (Prep)	2:08–2:50	**Core 5**	2:08–2:50	**Core 5**	2:08–2:50	6

The 10-period block schedule illustrated on the previous page demonstrates how to fit the four core academic programs of math, science, language arts, and social studies, as well as two periods of exploratory arts, into the school day. The extra blocks of time, the Core 5 period and the flex-time, are used by the team to provide for the special needs of children without excluding or limiting the time any child would spend in the general education and exploratory program. This flexibility provides teachers the opportunity (and the responsibility) to tailor the learning process and the time needed to individual students in order to maximize their learning.

Reading the schedule from left to right, each grade level is listed across the top of the schedule, with the exploratory arts programs in the right-hand column. All grade levels take their exploratory arts classes at their assigned two periods. During these two exploratory periods, the core academic teachers and the intervention specialists of IEP students have both a common planning period and a personal planning period.

The team planning time must be sacred time. Teams that meet parents during this time must reserve the first 10–15 minutes of the planning time for team planning, then schedule the parent-conference time. In schools with only one planning period per day, a rotating schedule by days of the week for personal and team planning time may work as an alternative.

> Note: All three grade levels start the day with a 35-minute activity period. This allows for intramurals and student activities as part of the regular school day. In today's world, neighborhood schools are a thing of the past, and transportation is a problem.
>
> When an activity period is included in the school day, students are given an opportunity to participate in clubs, intramurals, student councils, yearbook, etc. Without this period, many students would be excluded from this all-important time of early adolescent schooling. The flexible block schedule will be discussed in more detail in Chapter 7.

Mistake 9   **Modifications and/or accommodations are not clearly stated on the IEP.**

All accommodations and modifications need to be written on the IEP. The IEP is a working document that is to be used not only by the special education teacher, but also by the regular education teacher. General education teachers may struggle to develop modifications and accommodations for special needs students in the regular classroom. The intervention specialist teacher on the other hand, has been trained in how to make the modifications and accommodations necessary for the special needs students.

The properly implemented middle school model is again an important asset. When teachers teach in isolation, their view of the learning process is limited to only what they know and teach. However, when teachers teach in a team situation, the knowledge base is expanded by the number of teachers on the team. A common planning time allows the teachers to discuss the curriculum concepts to be taught and to share ideas for teaching and learning strategies that have been successful for student learning.

When intervention specialists are added to the teams, they add appropriate recommendations for accommodations and modifications to fit each specific student's needs. The practice of co-teaching allows the content teacher the opportunity to be the content expert, while the intervention specialist is the expert on accommodations and modifications of the curriculum. A strong partnership enhances the learning process for all students.

This is a time to look ahead. If a member of the IEP team foresees that a student will need an accommodation to successfully complete state assessments, that accommodation should be written into the IEP, and must be used throughout the year in the regular education classroom. In other words, for the student to be able to use an accommodation during assessment testing, the student must have used that accommodation in regular classroom work.

 **Mistake 10**

Prior written notice is not provided to a parent when there is a disagreement on identification, placement, or the provision of a Free and Appropriate Public Education (FAPE)

When there is a disagreement between the school district and the parents, the school is required to give prior written notice to the parents. The parents have a right to file a complaint or due process document to challenge what the school has offered as FAPE for their child. The elements that must legally be included in the FAPE notice are set forth in Section 615 if the IDEIA.

The easiest way to avoid the ten most common mistakes in IEP writing is through communication. When teachers and parents communicate with each other in their team planning sessions, they are better able to provide the best learning environment for all students. The proper implementation of the middle school teaming process enhances this success for all students. Accepting the idea that parents are partners is the key to understanding and the development of a trusting relationship. A true middle school opens its arms to parents in order to form these partnerships. The middle school philosophy works like a magic wand to reduce and eliminate the mysteries of differentiated instruction through communication, teacher teams, parental involvement, and flexible scheduling.

Chapter 6

The Secret of Middle School Scheduling

How can one schedule meet the needs of all students?

The Importance of the Middle School Schedule
● ●

Building the master schedule for a middle level school must be approached with caution. First, a list of priorities for the middle school components must be made. This list becomes the vision of the school program. The program goals are what drive the development or visioning process and should be based on the assessment of all students' needs and research-based best practices. Once the components of the program are identified and decided, a schedule must be developed that will support their implementation.

Many school buildings today are middle schools in name only because their schedules fail to support the middle school components. Truly changing more than the name over the door to "Middle School" requires altering the teaching methods and the organizational structure of teachers and students and their daily movement throughout the building. The master schedule of the school is critical to this metamorphosis—it must allow each middle school component to function in unison with the others.

Teacher Certification and the Middle School Schedule

Because the middle school level of education falls between the elementary and secondary levels of the educational structure, the middle school had no place of its own. Educators and students were, and often still are, treated as an extension of the elementary or secondary level. Traditionally teachers were trained as either elementary or high school teachers. Both of these certifications can be accommodated at the middle level since there is a grade overlap between sixth and eighth grade in most state certification plans. Also, in most states elementary certificates include the eighth-grade level, and the high school certificates begin at seventh grade and cover through the twelfth grade. This allows teachers who hold elementary certificates to teach through the eighth-grade level and secondary-certified teachers to teach as low as seventh grade.

An elementary certificate is a "generalist" certificate, since a single elementary teacher teaches math, science, social studies, language arts, and more. Secondary certificates are more content-specific and have a concentration in one of the core subjects (math, science, social studies, language arts) or a related arts area. Elementary teachers traditionally are certified through sixth grade, with secondary certificates covering teachers in junior highs, seventh through ninth grade, and the high school grades of 10 through 12. This overlap of certification in sixth and seventh grade has been *beneficial* to school districts that are losing students due to shifting populations or because of the mobility of today's society.

Middle School—
The "Hand-Me-Down" Level of Education

Often school districts find that they have a "surplus" of teachers at one particular level. The middle school provides an easy solution to this dilemma. Districts and schools can avoid certification problems with teachers being out-of-field or solve the *highly qualified* stipulations of NCLB by simply shifting teachers from elementary or high schools to the middle level. Is it any wonder that teachers at the middle school level are often referred to as the *stepchildren* of both the elementary and high schools since their assignments are primarily based on district staffing needs?

The fact that the middle school level has not been recognized as a separate entity in the educational process, and that teachers have not received specific training in teaching and meeting the developmental and academic needs of early adolescents, has created the mistaken assumption that the middle grades can be taught in the same manner and fashion as elementary or high school grades. Yet the pedagogy for the middle grades is different than that for the elementary or secondary grades. Teacher preparation for the elementary and secondary levels does not, in most cases, cover the specific needs and characteristics of the middle grades child and/or middle grade children with special needs. Neither elementary nor secondary pedagogy contains inclusion as part of the basic education curriculum, except for the limited special education training provided to pre-service teachers. This is very evident as one observes teachers trained at either the elementary or secondary levels.

This *stepchild* perception may also be rooted in the fact that the middle school was seen as a replacement for the junior high school. Whatever its cause, the perception has severely limited the development of good middle school programs and components for early adolescent students and children with special needs. When any level of school is staffed with teachers who are not trained for that level or don't want to be there, it is difficult to implement positive change. If middle schools continue to be the recipient of *extra* teachers because of budget cuts or the requirements of NCLB, they will remain middle schools in name only. In order to implement the components of middle level education as recommended in NMSA's *This We Believe*, and the National Forum's *Accelerating Change in Middle Grades Education*, middle level schools must become a priority for every district.

Middle School—
The Last "Best Chance" for American Education
• •

With the demand for educational improvements for all children, including students with special needs, some educators recognize middle schools as the last best chance for saving the failing American educational system. Middle level schools represent the last frontier to effect a change in the development of early adolescent students. The high school level may be too late in the education process of students, and students may not be ready at the elementary level. Today's challenge is great, especially in the present climate of negative press and testing as the only acceptable measurement of student achievement.

Examine when most students begin to lose interest in school. It begins in third to fifth grade. If the middle level of education does not motivate children to learn by providing an engaging curriculum that is meaningful to them, schools will continue to have students who are tuned out and turned off to learning. Educators lose students because they often are not in tune with where students are in the education process. In order to educate students, teachers must know how they learn, what their individual needs are, and what interests them. There are many reasons why this lack of understanding on the part of teachers and principals exists.

- The primary cause is the adherence to the period-by-period schedule and the ability grouping of students.

The period-by-period schedule was adopted from the high schools, passed down to junior highs, and remains today in a majority of middle schools. Periods determined by a number of minutes cannot accommodate variances in learning time for students. Research has demonstrated that children learn at different rates, yet this time period approach to learning persists.

The development of middle schools and the team structure—teams of teachers who have the same students and plan together—began eliminating the use of bells or music to signify the period change and restructured the time blocks for academic instruction. The flexible block schedule, as it has come to be known, is very popular in schools that have implemented the middle school model. Teachers have freedom to group and regroup students and to manipulate blocks of learning time. Teachers can utilize these flexible blocks to provide the small group instruction that some special needs students require to progress in the general education curriculum.

- A second reason teachers and administrators are not in tune with how and why students learn is the adherence to ability grouping of students and the exclusion of special needs students from the basic education classroom.

Ability grouping has allowed teachers to teach to only one ability level of students per class. Even when students of the same ability level are placed in a class, research shows that the students learn at different rates. Therefore, "one size" does not "fit all."

The grouping of special needs students in pullout classes is another form of ability grouping. IDEA legislation requires an end to this practice. NCLB focuses on the academic achievement of all students. The true middle school model utilizes teacher teams that include a special needs teacher, provides common planning time for the teacher teams, and operates with a flexible block schedule. This is the best way to serve all early adolescent children, including those who have specific services and supports required in their IEPs.

Building a Flexible Block Schedule

Building the master schedule must be done with caution. Several decisions must be made prior to its development. The schedule must be designed to allow the teachers and other staff the opportunity (time and flexibility) to meet all students' needs. How the schedule is built determines the degree of success the school will have in meeting this goal. Some of the items that should be decided before the scheduling process begins are:

1. How will teachers be assigned to teams?

2. How much planning time will they have?

3. How will the students be assigned to the teams?

4. How much freedom will teachers have with assigning students to academic classes (group and regrouping)?

5. How much flexibility will teachers have to adjust the core time blocks for teaching and learning?

6. What are the roles of the general education teacher and the intervention specialist on the same team?

7. How will students be identified for the inclusion program?

8. Will there be self-contained classes for those students who cannot be mainstreamed?

Use these questions as checkpoints for careful planning in developing a master schedule for an inclusive middle school with a flexible block schedule.

An Analysis of Question One
How will teachers be assigned to teams?

Teacher team assignment, either in an established school or in the creation of teams for a new school, is a critical factor for the school's success. The degree of success or failure in a middle school hinges on the quality of the working relationship and flexibility of the teacher teams. Therefore, teams become the heart of the middle school and need to be given a great deal of thought before formation.

Implementing change in an established middle level school where teachers have been together for many years can be just as difficult as establishing teams in a new middle school. This is often difficult since administrators need input and collaboration from teachers; yet, biases must be eliminated at all costs.

Administrators can observe the action of a team and identify individual teacher behaviors, skills, and work styles. It is also important to learn how each individual behaves and utilizes his or her skills as they work together in teaming situations. No decisions should be made on only one factor. Consideration should be given to as many objective factors as possible. Several pieces of data concerning each teacher must be examined:

- What does each individual bring to the team?

- How does the behavior and skill of an individual enable or hinder the team to act as a cohesive and effective unit?

Note: The team must maximize each team member's strength and compensate for any one team member's weakness in order to be a solid working group.

– A Note from Santo –

When you begin to examine how to place people on teams, subjectivity must be held in check. Objectivity in teacher assignment must be the guiding force when forming interdisciplinary teams.

How Teachers Were Placed on Teams at Grant Middle School

The objective process of gathering data about teachers for the purpose of assigning them to teams became a priority. In placing teachers on teams, several pieces of data were collected in order to make these decisions as objective as possible. As I mentioned in a previous chapter, the board-approved transition plan was very specific in how teacher and students were to be assigned to teams and houses. The teachers from the three previous middle schools were to be spread across the four houses of the new Grant Middle School. The intent of the plan was to create new affiliations and identities in the four houses of the new school and to eliminate the loyalty, traditions, and cultures entrenched within the three old schools. In order to apply the requirements dictated by the transition plan, I used the following process to place the teachers on teams:

- I observed teachers in a classroom setting.
- Teachers completed a Gregorc Style Delineator, a self-reporting teacher survey on:
  - how they believed they taught,
  - their classroom management style,
  - what subject they wanted to teach, and
  - who they wanted to team with, and not team with.

The observation instrument I used was developed from the Florida Performance Measurement System Summative Instrument, which recognizes effective research-based teaching strategies. Each teacher on a voluntary basis completed this Gregorc Style Delineator. Their classroom management and teaching styles were determined by their completed survey and confirmed by observation. The subjects they wanted to teach and the individuals they wanted to team with all came from their survey responses.

Data was entered into a FileMaker Pro Program and weighted. Data fields included:

- School where teacher taught in the previous year (Baker, Edison, Taft)
- Subjects teacher preferred to teach
- Gregorc Style Delineator classification of style
      CS—Concrete Sequential
      AS—Abstract Sequential
      AR—Abstract Random
      CR—Concrete Random
- Number of effective teaching strategies observed in classroom
      5 high, 1 low
- Teacher self-rating of teaching style
          4—Student Collaboration
          3—Combination (mostly Student Collaboration)
          2—Combination (mostly Direct Instruction)
          1—Direct Instruction

- *Teacher self-rating on preferred management styles*
    - *3—Facilitating*
    - *2—Student-centered with teacher input*
    - *1—Teacher-centered*

- *Preferred Teachers to Team With*

- *Preferred Teachers Not to Team With*

The data program was designed to spread the teachers across the houses starting with the category of the school the teacher last taught in, and moving down the list in the order as they are listed above. It distributed the teachers from the three schools as evenly as possible across the four houses. Next, it placed teachers according to subject preference and certification across the grade levels. It then assigned teachers by their Style Delineator score from CS, AS, AR, and CR, across the four houses, as well as by their classroom observation scores and self-ratings of teaching and management style. After the computer completed its work, we examined the list of teachers and their preferences for teammates. The only problem we encountered was that all union representatives were assigned to the same house (which we adjusted). Not everyone was able to serve on a team with everyone they had requested, but no one was teamed with an individual they did not want to team with. Throughout the year there were problems, as any first year situation might have, but not one major problem arose from the team assignments.

An Analysis of Question Two
How much planning time will the teams have?

Planning time is crucial to the success of a middle school team and program. With the lack of financial support for middle school programs, most districts treat the middle level like high school—with only one planning period a day. Teachers share neither common planning time nor students, defeating the purpose of teaming. Unfortunately, in schools that do provide common planning, teachers often do not know how (or refuse) to meet to accomplish what a good middle school team of teachers must do to support their students.

Two planning periods are needed if teachers are expected to provide the necessary program implementation, parent and teacher meetings, modifications and accommodations required to meet the individual needs of their students. In schools where only one planning period is possible, common planning for the team of core academic teachers and the special needs teacher is crucial if inclusion programs are to be successful. In those schools, perhaps time before or after school can be arranged and front-loaded to the morning for a daily extra period at least once or twice a week. If all else fails, lunchtime and periods before and after school can be used for common meeting times. This option, however, takes a heavy toll on teachers and burnout can occur very quickly. Remember: common planning is a must, and teachers must share students daily, or at least several times weekly.

An Analysis of Question Three
How will students be assigned to the teams?

Students should be assigned to teams in as equitable a manner as possible. Each team should have students of mixed abilities. Special needs students should be spread evenly among the teams in the same grade level. The same goes for students with behavior and attendance problems, and other special needs, such as limited English and giftedness. Often the temptation is to place the special students, problem students, or gifted students in separate classrooms. If you are dealing with large numbers and short staffing, this option may look very inviting to the school's leadership team. Also, often parents want their children in class only with certain other groups. Administrators who give in to this kind of pressure open the door for a select few, but will find they can never satisfy everyone.

Placing Students on Teams and in Houses at Grant Middle School

Creating the new Grant Middle School meant reassigning 1,300 students to four houses in the new building. The transition plan called for students to be spread evenly across the houses of the school in a manner reflecting the demographics of the community. This meant that students from the three original schools would be mixed and assigned to houses where they would have to make new friends and face new teachers.

Again, we utilized a FileMaker Pro Program to accomplish the task of placing the students. The first task was to move the fifth graders to the original middle school they would have normally attended as sixth graders. The current sixth graders and seventh graders at each of the existing middle schools were moved up a grade level. The students were then divided into groups based on the following:

- *Grade*
- *Middle school student would have attended*
- *Gender*
- *Ethnicity*
- *Grade-point average*
- *Days student was absent last school year*
- *Total days student was suspended in and out of school*

The computer assigned the students to grade level houses as evenly as possible, considering first the grade level, then the school they attended, or would have attended for sixth grade. The gender, ethnicity, grade-point average, number of days absent, and days suspended were all examined in their listed order as students were placed in the house and grade level assignments. The students with special needs were distributed across the houses as evenly as possible after all other students were placed. Students stayed with their assigned houses for their entire middle school experience. Guidance counselors were assigned by grade level and moved along with the children up through the grades.

During the second year of operation, finances forced the Board of Education to reduce the number of administrators from four to three. As a result, each became a principal for one of the sixth, seventh, and eighth grades and continued "rolling up" with that group of students as they moved through the grades.

An Analysis of Question Four
How much freedom will teachers have in assigning students to academic classes, grouping, and regrouping?

In order for inclusion to work and meet the needs of all students, teachers must have the flexibility to group and regroup students on a regular basis. There are times when teachers may want students grouped for a certain learning activity and then regrouped for another. Teachers know best what students' needs are. Giving them the authority and responsibility to group and regroup students for instruction allows students who are accelerating to move ahead while those that need extra work time on a topic to remain. As long as students are not left in the same group for extended periods of time, grouping and regrouping provides flexibility to extend the learning experience based on the individual needs of students. The building schedule can either limit or enhance the teachers' ability to move students around during the core academic time.

An Analysis of Question Five

How much flexibility will teachers have in adjusting the core time blocks for teaching and learning?

The schedule must be designed so that two or three core time blocks are placed back-to-back. This permits the teachers to adjust the learning time among themselves and their respective subjects as needed. The only time that students are not with their team of teachers is during lunch and the two exploratory classes. In addition, building one or two extra periods in the schedule provides flexible time for the core academic teachers to extend academic learning time into one or both of these blocks. This allows extra learning time for academic acceleration or remediation based on individual students' needs. Extra periods may also be used to accommodate an exploratory overload.

One such exploratory overload was the music program at Grant Middle School. The flexible schedule allowed for two exploratory blocks, but students were permitted to take up to three music classes. Since only two class periods of the day allowed for exploratory, and orchestra was the smallest music program, we offered orchestra during flex time. This allowed students to accommodate all of their music classes and still have other exploratory experiences such as technology, television production, and physical education. Physical education, chorus, and band were offered on a rotating day basis.

Adding extra periods in the schedule requires creating more, shorter periods. A rotating day schedule (often called an A-Day, B-Day schedule) actually provides more academic learning time than a regular period-by-period schedule and more exploratory course offerings in a three-, six-, or nine-week session. The important thing to remember is that by investing teachers with as much schedule flexibility as possible, they can be creative in insuring that their students have the best program possible, with a variety of academic and exploratory offerings.

An Analysis of Question Six

What are the roles of the general education teacher and the intervention specialist?

It is imperative that both the general education teacher and the intervention specialist, both professional educators, work together in the inclusion classroom.

The true value of having the intervention specialist in the same room with the general education teacher can be limited by the relationship and lack of understanding of the two roles. General education teachers may feel uncomfortable with another teacher in their classroom. Some intervention specialists perform more as an aide whose only function is to duplicate class materials and work only with special needs students who are included in the general education classroom.

The general education teacher and the intervention specialist must understand the concept of co-teaching and feel comfortable with the process. This may require inservice training. In an inclusion classroom, the basic education teacher is responsible for the content that is being taught. The intervention specialist is responsible for modifying and adjusting the content so that special needs students will fully understand it. In other words, the general education teacher is responsible for the *what* of the lesson, and the intervention specialist is responsible for the *how*. The teachers must be given common time to design and plan lessons if all students' needs are to have the best chance of being met. In a successfully co-taught classroom, it is difficult to tell who the general education teacher is and who the intervention specialist is, since they are both engaged in teaching and assisting students. The same is true for the students in the classroom, because all students are receiving assistance in the learning process.

Staff development in differentiated instruction is essential. General education teachers must be trained in using appropriate teaching strategies. Modifications by the intervention specialist must be implemented to meet the expectations for the special needs students. Teachers must have a high level of trust in order to effectively co-teach in the same classroom. If teachers are not planning and working together, it is difficult to establish this level of trust.

An Analysis of Question Seven
How will students be identified for the inclusion program?

Any student who has been identified as a special needs student and who has an IEP may participate in the regular classroom. Special needs students will participate and make progress in the general curriculum with the help of the intervention specialist. All students benefit from having both the general education teacher and the intervention specialist in the same classroom. Many general education students who do not qualify for special education services may benefit from the strategies the intervention specialist brings to the classroom. These students can receive the special services in a co-teaching setting.

An Analysis of Question Eight
Will there be self-contained classes for special needs students who cannot be mainstreamed?

There should be self-contained classes for special need students who cannot be mainstreamed, however, all students should be mainstreamed whenever possible. The goal is that all students receive appropriate instruction in the least restrictive environment.

An Analysis of Question Nine
What will the flexible block schedule look like?

The master schedule of a high-functioning middle school must give teachers the opportunity to make decisions concerning the learning activities for students on a daily basis. Teachers should have the freedom to make decisions concerning the time length of the learning blocks and the way students are grouped for instruction. There are many factors that the teaching team must adjust on an ongoing basis. If the teaming skills are developed and the schedule allows for the grouping and regrouping of students, then teams can meet the individual needs of students.

Building extra blocks of time into the schedule allows for adjustments during the day. The blocks can be used to provide extra learning time to accommodate students who are accelerating, as well as those students who need additional time on a topic. Often people consider the number of minutes in an eight- or nine-period day too short for adequate learning. However, when they realize that the extra blocks of time are used to extend learning time in academic subjects, they see that the schedule allows for the possibility of more accessible learning time.

In the schedule below (similar to one on page 68), there is for each grade level an extra period *(Core 5)* of academic time that the team of teachers can utilize for added learning time. The *flex* time is used to offer students who are taking multiple music courses the opportunity to participate in band or orchestra or both. Students not registered in multiple music classes or not taking band or orchestra, can be scheduled for extra academic time during the flex period.

Grant Middle School Flexible Block Schedule

6th Grade		7th Grade		8th Grade		Encore Teachers	
8:10–8:45 (35)	Activity	8:10–8:45	Activity	8:10–8:45	Activity	8:10–8:45	Activity
8:45–9:27 (42)	Core 1	8:45–9:27	Core 1	8:45–9:27	Rel. Arts (Team)	8:45–9:27	8
9:27–10:09 (42)	Core 2	9:27–10:09	Core 2	9:27–10:09	Rel. Arts (Prep)	9:27–10:09	8
10:09–10:50 (41)	**Flex**	10:09–10:51	Core 3	10:09–10:51	Core 1	10:09–10:50	Team
10:50–11:20 (30)	**Lunch**	**10:51–11:32 (41)**	**Flex**	10:51–11:33	Core 2	10:50–11:20	Lunch
11:20–12:02 (42)	Core 3	**11:32–12:02 (30)**	**Lunch**	**11:33–12:14 (41)**	**Flex**	11:20–12:02	Prep
12:02–12:44 (42)	Core 4	12:02–12:44	Rel. Arts (Team)	**12:14–12:44 (30)**	**Lunch**	12:02–12:44	7
12:44–1:26 (42)	**Core 5**	12:44–1:26	Rel. Arts (Prep)	12:44–1:26	Core 3	12:44–1:26	7
1:26–2:08 (42)	Rel. Arts (Team)	1:26–2:08	Core 4	1:26–2:08	Core 4	1:26–2:08	6
2:08–2:50 (42)	Rel. Arts (Prep)	2:08–2:50	**Core 5**	2:08–2:50	**Core 5**	2:08–2:50	6

Please Note:

- All grade level teams have four core teachers and one special education teacher who share students and common planning.
- This schedule allows for a 35-minute activity period daily for all grades.
- Each grade has five 42-minute blocks of core time.
- The grade level team decides how the students move through the core classes.
- Teachers use the fifth core period at their discretion. It can be used for reading across the subject areas, academic acceleration, or remediation.
- Each grade level has a flex period of 41 minutes. This accommodates an overload of courses in the exploratory program. For example, in the Grant

Middle School situation many students took all three music classes—band, orchestra, and chorus. Seventy percent of the students took chorus. Therefore, chorus and physical education were offered during one of the exploratory periods per grade level. Students taking chorus would receive instruction in chorus on Monday, Wednesday, and Friday, and take physical education on Tuesday and Thursday. The balance of the students would be assigned to general music on Tuesday and Thursday, with physical education on Monday, Wednesday, and Friday. Students taking band or orchestra were scheduled on a rotating day schedule during the flex period by grade level. In this manner, some students took as many as three music classes and still had the time to take other exploratory classes in the remaining exploratory period.

The Importance of the Exploratory Program

Early adolescent students need exposure to as many exploratory classes as possible. Often parents are misled in thinking that their children should begin to specialize at an early age in music, athletics, and art. Research shows some students develop faster than others. Therefore, allowing children to experience as many of the related arts as possible before they specialize in one provides them with a knowledge and experience base upon which to make future choices. Students will make better class choices as they move into high school because of the exposure they have had in middle school. There is no doubt that the arts contribute to learning and the human experience. The middle school's job is to provide exposure before specialization.

An exploratory program should be built on just that—exploration. Early adolescent children need hands-on experiences. Exploratory classes do not have to be semester or yearlong sessions, especially at the sixth-grade level. Students should be rotated through all exploratory classes at the sixth-grade level, with some choices at seventh- and more choices at eighth-grade level. Three-week, six-week, and nine-week wheels should be included in the schedule, especially at the sixth-grade level. Semester choices could be offered in seventh grade, and both semester and yearlong courses in eighth grade. This will provide students with a wealth of exploratory experience and allow them to have choices as they move up the grades.

Chapter 7

A Final Note: One Success Story

What can educators learn from the Grant Middle School experience?

This chapter will discuss the steps educators must take in establishing an inclusion program that is successful in meeting the needs of all children in the context of an actual middle school.

The Advocate's View

Working on the inclusion program at Grant Middle School was a rewarding experience for me as a mother and as an advocate. Everything about the middle school concept fit with the fight I had been waging over the years for my own child and other children all over Ohio. When Dr. Piño approached me in an effort to get parents involved in the transition plan for Grant Middle School, I was intrigued. The more he talked about the program, the more

excited I got. This was truly an administrator who actually *got it*.

I was not familiar with the Middle School concept. I had only read about it. Many of the so-called middle schools where I worked as an advocate were really just junior high schools and not at all conducive to children with special needs. Dr. Piño walked me through the transition plan and asked for my support with parents within the community. I sincerely believed in what he was trying to

(continued)

accomplish at Grant. Now, a year later, after the opening of Grant Middle School and working with the teams of teachers, administrators, and parents, I can say "IT WORKS."

I can say this with confidence as a result of a conversation I had with a young lady in sixth grade at Grant last spring. I asked her how she liked Grant Middle School. She said that at first she was scared. She came from a school with 400 students, and Grant had 1,350, but the four-house concept made things a lot easier. I asked her how she felt about having special needs kids in her class. She stated that she didn't know who was in special education and who was not. There were two teachers in the classroom to help whoever needed help, so it didn't matter. I almost cried. That is what every parent of a child with special needs wants for his or her child—the opportunity to be just like everyone else.

Taking it to the Community

Once you have built your critical mass of support for implementation, you will need to make sure all of the community is involved. Currently, with federal and state financial resources continually decreasing, community involvement takes on a more significant meaning. Community involvement can make or break any success a school system may be trying to achieve. No longer is just the community's buy-in important; you will also need the community's financial support.

There are five components to getting community involvement, and they are:

B — Bring lead agencies and community leaders together.

U — Understand what they do.

Y — You are key to success through education and follow-through.

I — Involve parents.

N — Never give up.

Step One

Bring Lead Agencies and Community Leaders Together

Look within your community and identify the agencies that support families. Find out who the shakers and the movers of the community are. Think outside the box. Ask, "Who sets up community events?" Here are just a few agencies to begin your list.

- Job and Family Services
- Children's Services

— *(continued)* —

- United Way
- Boy Scouts
- Girl Scouts
- Church leaders
- 4-H Club leaders
- Doctors
- Nurses
- Teachers
- CEOs of industry
- Clubs such as Knights of Columbus
- Mental health boards
- Lawyers
- Publishers of local newspapers
- Juvenile court judges
- Ministers
- Priests
- Business owners

This list is endless. Each community is different. Begin your own list today.

Step Two

Understand What They Do

Once you have identified all of the agencies within the community, you will have to find out what they do. An agency like Job and Family Services connects needy families with programs and resources in an effort to help them become self-sufficient. United Way supports numerous organizations in the community that in turn support families in multiple areas of need.

Ask yourself:

- What areas of family needs do each of these organizations address in their mission statement?
- How can this support what is happening in the school?

Step Three

You Are the Key—Educate and Follow Through

After you have identified the community agencies and their missions, think about how you can be a support to the community. Then find a way to educate them.

Set up a community meeting over lunch. Make it a simple, paper bag lunch. Everyone brings their own lunch; you provide the place and drinks. Have an agenda. Start and end on time. Community leaders are busy people, and you do not want to waste their time. These meetings are set up to form subgroups. These subgroups will focus on certain areas of the transition plan.

- Briefly explain the program.
- Let each one know what is in it for them.
- Give them the opportunity to be part of the program.

(continued)

- Get names of agencies who will be willing to be a part of the program.

Step Four

Involve Parents

Parents can be wonderful assets, but you must make them feel valued. Open your doors and invite parents into the school. Talk with parents and find out if they would like to be part of a group of key community leaders. Try and get as many parents involved as possible. Parents from diverse groups make the best resources.

After you have identified parents that can bring something to your subgroups, arrange for them to attend a meeting. Have each subgroup set up an action plan. Try to know up front who your *talkers* are and who your *doers* are.

Ask yourself:
- What is the subgroup's mission?
- Who will do what?

Step Five

Never Give Up

Getting community buy-in is not an easy task. It takes someone who does not need constant back-patting and positive reinforcement. Unfortunately, the community, in general, focuses only on negativity. It is up to the school district, agencies, organizations, and involved parents to get the positive aspects of education out to the public.

Have an open house at school to celebrate all students and their successes. Make sure student projects are on display within the community. The more the school is seen outside of its own four walls, the more the impact will be felt throughout the community. It will not happen overnight, but it will happen.

Once programs in the school system become an asset to agencies, organizations, and parents within the community, it is time to start asking for financial support. When the program has solid outcome data that supports it is good for the community, it is time to ask for support for the school. The community can provide support by investing capital, providing in-kind matching funds for donations, writing support letters for grant applications, or supporting school levies.

If you want to be community-supported, let your community know how you are making their lives easier and better. Remember, "Toot your own horn"; it takes seven positives to offset one negative.

The Administrator's View

The middle school model properly implemented provides the best chance for achieving a successful inclusion program. There are several reasons for this, but the primary ones are:

- the teaming of teachers,
- common planning,
- grouping and regrouping, and
- a flexible schedule.

It is important to note that the middle school model will work at the other levels of schooling, the elementary and high school levels, just as well. Elementary schools often team teachers by grade level at the primary level, and by interdisciplinary teams at the intermediate grades. High schools are beginning to team teachers, especially at the ninth grade level, often for the purpose of creating advisory groups or providing curriculum in career clusters. The name of the teaming process is not the important issue; the fact that teachers are meeting together to share information and support all students is the important factor.

Change efforts are starting to occur either through the school improvement process or the need to comply with state and federal mandates, all of which must begin with an idea of the final goal in mind. A vision for what success will look like once the change has been implemented should be the driving force behind any change effort. This vision is often that of the building principal or a school district. Regardless of who has the vision, a process must be followed to implement the vision.

Putting It All Together

I was responsible for developing an inclusion program that included all students at the Manatee Education Center in Naples, Florida. Manatee was a K-8 center. Their program focused on inclusion of all specials needs students

(continued)

(including the non-English speaking students), in the basic education program. Houses (schools-within-a-school) and teacher-student looping (long-term student/teacher progression) were two important components of the school's organization. I also developed an inclusion program for Grant Middle School in Marion, Ohio. The Marion plan called for combining three existing middle schools into one school, with four equal houses. Personnel and students from the three existing schools were mixed evenly in the four new houses at one facility. Each house would have an equal distribution of special needs students included in the general education program. Each house was to be representative of the demographics of the community.

In the case of the Manatee Center, I was asked by the superintendent to research the current literature on educating children of elementary and middle school age and to design the particular focus for the program. In the case of the Grant Middle School, I was hired by the district as director of middle school programs, and given a plan that was developed through a research of

literature by a committee of middle grades teachers and administrators with the assistance of a consultant. In both situations, the research produced two common elements that were contained in the plans:

1. a program that would include the special needs students in the basic education classrooms

2. the creation of small learning communities in the larger school community

In both plans, the initial vision for the change process was developed by small groups within the school structure. In both cases, the vision had to be created and shared by a large group of stakeholders if buy-in for the plans was to become a reality. The following is a description of how the visions for the plans were shared.

Step One
The Vision

Every plan begins with the vision of what success will look like. In all cases, in order for the vision of a planned change to move forward, it must be shared with others who are stakeholders and whose support is

(continued)

needed if the change is to be attained. These individuals become the *visioning team.*

The visioning team identifies additional individuals in the school system and the community at large who are *centers of influence* (COI). The COI can either promote the vision or block it from becoming a reality. It is imperative that all such individuals be identified, and that the groups these COI represent are included in the change process.

The COI are introduced to the vision. The visioning team gathers and analyzes their input and reactions. Then the vision is adjusted in response to their recommendations. As a leader of any change process, it is important to understand that in order for a vision to move forward, and buy-in to occur, the vision must be adjusted to meet a level of acceptance from all COI.

Understand that the COI may not always accept the proposed change; the visioning team will still need to work with them. The negative COI must be strategically positioned so they cannot destroy the plan. They should be given assignments that are meaningful to accomplish the common goal. The idea is to spread the negative influences so they can't become a critical force able to destroy the plan.

Remember, you want to involve the negative people in positive ways. If they are part of the process, it is hard for them to criticize the effort. As the saying goes, "Keep your friends close, and your enemies even closer."

Know your research. Always have research available to support your plan. This will help quiet the concerns of the naysayer. You might not be able to totally convince them, but they are less likely to speak up if they know you know what you are talking about.

Step Two
Taking Your Plan to The Community

Once the COI are indentified and formed into larger teams, hold meetings in the community to acquaint others with the plan. In many cases these meetings are better held at sites away from the school so that parents and

(continued)

community members feel safe and comfortable.

The concept here is to take the school to the community, in other words meet them on their turf. All community groups, including parents (especially those with children of special needs), church clergy, civic organizations, and service clubs, need to be mobilized in order to get the message of the planned change out to the public. Meetings need to be held with parents and teachers of students who will be attending the new school so they understand what is being planned for them.

Don't forget to include the students. They also need to understand the vision and to buy into the change process. Let them know the benefits of the plan for them as students. Parents like having happy children. Even if they don't quite understand the plan, if their children believe in it, they will still support it.

It is a good idea to set up presentations for different groups so that they follow the same format and language. It is important to talk with a united voice and use the same message points. In this manner, the message that is being delivered about the plan is the same, regardless of who is saying it. It is crucial that the

scope and limitations of the change are specified to the community. In essence, the limits of the plan must be spelled out so there is no doubt about the intent of the plan. Everyone needs to know and understand what can and cannot be done within the limits of the plan.

This is an important step because once the vision for the plan is released, assumptions will be made about what is to happen, and the *rumor mill* will begin. If this phase of the process is not controlled properly, those who want to stop the proposal will have the greatest chance to build a negative force to destroy the effort. Utilize your community leaders as vocal points for questions and answers. They can stop the rumor mill. Community members will listen and be influenced more by an organized group of their leaders than by single negative individuals.

Step Three
Soliciting Additional Input from The Community

Once your vision has been delivered to the community, the COI should monitor the response that occurs. They need to listen to the specific influence groups within their

(continued)

neighborhoods to be sure the correct message is getting out. They should be able to respond to any negative feedback that occurs.

Additional input received at community meetings needs to be brought forward. The visioning team can make adjustments as needed to the vision, thus creating a possibility of a larger buy-in. Remember, as you make your minor changes, you must always be faithful to the true mission of the plan and what is to be accomplished.

Before I was hired, the specifics of the Grant Middle School plan had been established by a "Transition Team" composed of teachers and administrators and approved by the board of education. Therefore, my role was to take the board-approved plan and implement it. Since school personnel had developed the plan, my first task was to share it with the stakeholders from the community. This included parents, community leaders, and service organizations within the city of Marion.

I planned a series of meetings at schools, service group gatherings, and senior citizen communities. In essence, I went anywhere I could speak to the community about the approved middle school plan.

During this time, I also developed community buy-in by recruiting individuals who wanted to be part of seven committees. These seven committees were created to address the seven major components recommended in the plan. The seven committees included:

- Curriculum
- Discipline
- Athletics/Intramurals
- Public Relations/Communication
- Advisory/Character Education
- Student Activities
- Internal Structure Houses/ Teaming/Scheduling/Planning

The purpose of the seven committees was to develop recommendations for successful implementation of the board's plan. The parameters approved by the board for the components of the new school were reviewed at each of these community meetings. It was made clear that the role of these seven committees was advisory in nature. In other words, the committees were not to change the plan, but to develop recommendations as to how the plan could be implemented.

(continued)

These community meetings were designed to get the approved plan to as many stakeholders as possible. I needed to meet as many people from the community as possible in order to get their input and, at the same time, provide an opportunity for parents and community members to be part of the process so that a critical mass of people who would support the effort could be established.

Most visioning efforts fail because the critical mass to sustain the effort is never reached. The ideal process for any situation would be to have parents and community members as part of the "Transition Team" at the start of the process. Attempting to get people on board after a planned change has been approved is much more difficult. I constantly had to work with parents and community members because they did not understand what was happening at the school. We spent a great deal of time reaffirming what the plan meant for the new building. The only saving grace was that we had two years to implement the plan before we opened the new school. This period provided adequate time to build a relationship with the stakeholders. We were able to form a critical mass of support for implementation of the program.

A Collaborative Effort Between the School and Community:

The implementation of middle school components differed in the three existing schools. All three schools had teacher teams, but common planning was not fully implemented in any of the schools. Teachers might have the same planning time, but planning meetings were not always structured or focused. None of the three schools had a flexible schedule, and some of the schools were still using bells to change periods. Special needs students were mostly in pullout programs or grouped together in certain classes, resulting in their exclusion, rather than inclusion. A review of the individual educational plans (IEPs) of special needs students, showed the majority were poorly written and not specific to individual student's needs. In classes that included special needs students, the resource teacher acted as an aide rather than a professional teacher. They ran off copies or provided one-on-one support for students (separated from the rest of the class). In essence, the schools were not organized to meet IDEA

— (continued) —

requirements from 1997 reauthorization. The test scores showed little to no progress. Only one of the three schools was meeting adequate yearly progress as required by NCLB.

The board-approved plan for the new school required that inclusive practices be implemented in the new school. Therefore, there was an urgent need for staff development. Teachers were not trained in differentiated instruction strategies, nor accustomed to having another professional in the room co-teaching with them.

Although the district staff development office began to offer differentiated instruction workshops, these efforts were limited because of a lack of funds. Grants were written, and the funds received provided staff development dollars to train teachers and pay them for their extra time and effort. A full year before the opening of the new school, consultants were brought in, and inservice training sessions were held. In addition, three student waiver days were requested from the state and approved so that teachers could focus on staff development activities and be paid for their time and efforts. Throughout the year, early dismissal days were used to allow for more training sessions on teaming skills and co-teaching strategies.

Since parent involvement was also vital to the success of the program, a partnership was developed between the school and Ms. Dena Hook, the director of Children and Family First Council, for the purpose of assisting in the development of a parent involvement program. The Family and Children Council Board is a collaboration of social service agencies in Marion County, and serves as a collective body to provide services and support for needy families. Ms. Hook's expertise was in special education, and she was engaged in her current position of providing services to many of the families whose children attended the schools. Over 95 percent of the children that she worked with had, or were suspected of having, some form of disability.

When we took the new school plan to the community, the largest group of parents with concerns about the program was the parents of children with disabilities. The proposed change would require these students to move from a traditional program of self-contained pullout programs to an inclusion program. Parents wanted to be assured that the needs of their children would be met with this new inclusion program. Ms. Hook's experience as an advocate, as

(continued)

a parent of a special needs child, and though her position of serving families in the community were key in getting parent acceptance and involvement in the program. In addition, her experience as a trainer, program director, and professional advocate in the area of special education was a valuable resource. Because she sat on the other side of the table as an advocate, and had been trained in the IEP process by Office of Special Education Program (OSEP) at the U.S. Department of Education, she was able to make valuable suggestions for our procedures and explain how IEPs were written. She conducted training sessions for the teacher teams on how to conduct parent conferences and how to write IEPs correctly.

Why It Works

The middle school concept and special education go hand in hand. America's school systems must start making changes to meet the needs of all children. NCLB and IDEIA are not going away. Implementing the middle school research-based best practices is the answer to success for children with special needs. The middle school model, correctly implemented, can easily accommodate students with special needs, allow teachers to work to provide learning time that they control, and tailor experiences to the needs of the students on their team. The model places control for the learning of all students in the hands of the teachers. If they are to be accountable, then they must control the learning. What better place for that control to be but in the classrooms! The community collaboration, established in the planning of the school's programs, has led to more community awareness. The community has discovered what it can do to support schools, teachers, and, most importantly, today's students.

Although the district has fallen on hard times financially, the community and teachers stand firm in protecting the middle school program components implemented at Grant Middle School. Teachers have worked together with the support of the community, despite no salary increases for three years consecutively. The middle school programs, which were developed over the last three years, remain in place while other district services have been cut or eliminated. The middle school program at Grant Middle School belongs to the entire community, not just the school system. It is embedded in the culture and people of Marion, Ohio.

Frequently Asked Questions

Questions for the Advocate:

QUESTION: *Must a school district evaluate a child if the parent requests an evaluation?*

ANSWER: The law states that when a child is suspected of having a disability, the local education agency (LEA) is required to evaluate. If the LEA does not suspect the child of having a disability, they are **not** required to evaluate even if the parent makes a request.

QUESTION: *Must a parent sign their child's IEP each year before the LEA can implement it?*

ANSWER: No. The only time a local education agency (LEA) requires the parent's signature is on the initial individualized education program (IEP) when the child is identified as having a disability. Once the LEA has the parent's permission to implement special education, the LEA is required to provide special education every year until the child tests out of special education. If a parent disagrees with the IEP, the only way to stop the implementation of that IEP is to file due process.

QUESTION: *Is inclusion mandated in the Individual with Disabilities Education Act of 1997 (IDEA)?*

ANSWER: The word "inclusion" is not written into the law; however, the term "least restrictive environment" (LRE) is written into the law.

QUESTION: *What is least restrictive environment?*

ANSWER: Least restrictive environment (LRE) is defined as education in the regular education classroom with the provision of appropriate services and supports.

QUESTION: *Can a parent dictate to a school district what methodology to use for a child with a disability?*

ANSWER: No. Parents cannot dictate methodology. But, the local education agency (LEA) must prove that the methodology they are using provides an appropriate education for the student and that the student is progressing in the general education curriculum.

QUESTION: *Is the building principal required to be present at the individualized learning program (IEP) meeting?*

ANSWER: No. The law states that a district representative who is knowledgeable about the curriculum and services available in the district and who can commit to those services must be present. If the special education director or anyone else representing the school fits this description, the local education agency (LEA) has met the requirements of the law.

QUESTION: *What should the school do if the parents cannot or will not attend the individualized learning program (IEP) meeting?*

ANSWER: Document, Document, Document. Make sure that you have sent an invitation to the parent with several different options for time and date. Make at least three different attempts to communicate with the parent regarding the IEP meeting. The law states that IEP meetings are to be set at a convenient time and place for all parties on the IEP team.
- Do **not** send an invitation home with the student.
- Do **not** leave a message on an answering machine.
- **Always** send invitations via the regular mail.
- **Always** speak directly with the parent and follow it up with a letter summarizing your conversation.

QUESTION: *Does the regular education teacher have a need to know what is written on the individualized learning plan (IEP)?*

ANSWER: Yes, in accordance with No Child Left Behind (NCLB) and the Individual with Disabilities Education Act of 1997 (IDEA), a child with a disability must progress in the general education curriculum. A regular education teacher must understand what accommodations or modifications or both are included on the IEP to assist them in providing an appropriate education for a child with a disability.

QUESTION: *Must regular education teachers provide accommodations and/or modifications specified on the individualized learning plan (IEP)?*

ANSWER: Yes. They are also required under the Rehabilitation Act of 1973, Section 504, to provide the services written on the IEP. Section 504 is a civil rights law that states that a child with a disability is entitled to the same education as a child without disabilities. Accommodations and modifications level the playing field for children with disabilities. Teachers who choose not to provide services such as accommodations and modifications can be sued under Section 504.

Questions for the Administrator:

QUESTION: *How do you allow for special need students who require more time to learn than the core academic time allows?*

ANSWER: There are only so many hours in the school day. Once you subtract lunch, planning time, passing time, etc., out of the total school day, you are left with the number of minutes for instruction of both core and exploratory classes. If you are teaching the four core classes of math, science, language arts, and social studies (or reading, if not included in language arts), and two exploratory classes, you need six blocks of instructional time. A seventh or eighth block of time can be added for students who require assistance for special needs or acceleration. This seventh or eighth block of time **is** additional academic time, and students who don't need the extra time may be grouped and regrouped for additional instruction. Additional time per subject can be added on a rotating basis by day of the week. The core team should control how these extra blocks of time are used. All teachers on the team are engaged in teaching during these time blocks. (See one master schedule on page 87.)

QUESTION: *How do you justify these shorter periods of learning time?*

ANSWER: The average attention span for an early adolescent is 10–12 minutes. Therefore, an activity change is needed three to four times during a 40- to 50-minute period. Middle school students have difficulty sitting for any length of time, so movement is important. Short focused learning periods are most effective for this age level. Shortening the periods and adding the two extra periods of instruction allows the team greater flexibility in meeting the particular learning needs of their students. Instruction is more focused, and you are servicing the normal physical need for change in this age group.

QUESTION: *How do you motivate teachers to change the way they teach and accept teaming?*

ANSWER: Teachers are no different than children. They need to be motivated to learn. We must provide incentives for teachers just as we do students. The best motivation for teachers, besides wanting to do a good job, is professional treatment and payment for their time and efforts. The payment does not always have to be in money. Teachers appreciate time off, recognition, and celebrations as well. Also taking some of the "must do" items away can help.

We have a bad habit of adding to the "must do" list for teachers and expecting them to continue with their current responsibilities as well. With today's accountability, they are becoming overrun with new tasks. The constant demands lead to resistance and burnout. Try reducing the stress of change by making the process more appealing; include teachers in the process. Remember, change is more readily accepted by the people who have helped to plan and implement it.

QUESTION: *How important is the school board's approval in the change process?*

ANSWER: The school board's approval is essential to the success of any change process. Everything dealing with the proposed change must be approved and accepted by the school board. Timing, training, practice with new skills, and community response must be thoroughly explained so the board will know what to expect. Just as today's advertisements for new medications list all of the possible side effects, you must prepare the school board for all possible issues, especially the negative ones. I have seen many good change projects go down in defeat, even after board approval, because of negative community reaction.

QUESTION: *How do you handle the teacher who just won't accept change?*

ANSWER: There will always be a few individuals against the change being suggested. Phillip Schlechty, in his book *Inventing Better Schools*, (pp 216–218), puts these individuals into two classes—*stay-at-homers* and *saboteurs*. The *stay-at-homers* will consider change only after all their friends accept it, and then only because they can't stand being alone. You can work with these individuals and eventually win them over. The *saboteurs*, on the other hand, seem to like being isolated and excluded and actually consider it an honor. The saboteurs probably will never accept change, and you must either live with them or arrange for a transfer. During the change process, leaders should always negotiate a way in which to deal with the saboteurs you will encounter.

QUESTION: *How do you get general education teachers and resource specialists to co-teach?*

ANSWER: Both teachers must have an understanding of their role in any co-teaching situation. The general education teacher must be responsible for the content of what is being taught. The resource specialist is responsible for supplying the strategies and accommodations that will level the playing field for the special needs student. Teachers must be given the necessary time and opportunity to work together and develop confidence in each other. Co-teaching is a skill that is built on the respect that teachers develop for each other over time.

QUESTION: *How do teachers grade the special needs students in the general education classroom?*

ANSWER: The grade for the student should be a collaborative effort by both the general education teacher and the resource teacher. They both need to examine the objectives of the content and be sure that instruction includes modifications and strategies needed by the student. Many districts utilize a comment section that follows the grade given a particular subject on the report card. Comments alert parents to the fact that the grade their child earned was at, above, or below grade level. This identifies for the parent their child's instructional performance level for the subject.

In grading, the important thing is how well the student understands and can apply the concepts learned to new situations. The point is not how well he or she does in comparison to other students in the class, but how well he or she understands the concept being taught. For example, if the concept is latitude and longitude for the basic education student, it may mean answering the question, "At what latitude and longitude does the state of Kentucky lie?" A special needs student in that same class may respond to the question, "At the corner of which streets is the post office located?" Both students who answer these types of questions correctly may receive an "A" for their grade. However, the basic education student's grade is at grade level, while the special education student's grade is below grade level. Both students applied this general education curriculum concept to the best of their ability.

QUESTION: *How do you handle the comments of educators that say, "But we've always done it this way!"*

ANSWER: Just because "we've always done it this or that way" does not make it right. We must base decisions on what research tells us is effective, and eliminate those practices that are not. For too long, we have supported practices of education for the wrong reasons. It takes courage to go against the tide of criticism and support what is right for our children. Be a brave and courageous leader and stand up for what's right for students.

Glossary

- **Ability Grouping**
  Ability Grouping is the practice of placing students in a learning group by ability for extended periods of time (a year or more). This practice restricts the students to only one learning environment and social interaction.

- **Academic Rigor**
  Academic rigor is instruction delivered with high expectations of student achievement.

- **Accommodations**
  Accommodations are whatever it takes to make sure that a student with disabilities can participate as fully as possible in the general education curriculum

- **AD/HD**
  Attention Deficit Disorder with and without hyperactivity

- **Basic Education Curriculum**
  The basic education curriculum is the course offerings that the state and local school board require all regular students to take each year.

- **Brain-based Facilitation**
  Teaching strategies that are aligned with the way the brain learns and functions.

- **Core Academic Classes**
  Core academic classes consist of language arts (reading), math, social studies, and science

- **Developmentally Appropriate Instruction**
  Instruction strategies and teaching methods that meet the physical, psychological, and mental development level of the student.

- **Exploratory/Related Arts/Encore Classes**
  All of these classes are supplemental to the basic core academic program. They are often offered on a wheel, with several courses operating on a 3-, 6-, 9-, or 18-week basis. There are a few of these courses that are offered on a yearlong basis. The purpose of these courses is to offer early adolescent students exposure to a variety of courses to determine their interests, which they can focus on high school.

- **FAPE**
  Free Appropriate Public Education—Special education and related services, which are provided at public expense, under public supervision and direction.

- **FBA**
  Functional Behavior Assessment is the process used to develop a behavior modification plan on an IEP

- **Flexible Block Schedule**
  The Flexible Block Schedule provides teachers and students a schedule for learning that can be altered on a daily or weekly basis, depending on the needs of the students. The only time blocks that remain fixed are periods when the students leave the team for lunch and exploratory courses.

- **Grouping and Regrouping Students**
  Grouping and regrouping students is the practice of placing students in different learning groups for instruction by the teacher team. This allows for students to be mixed by ability or learning activity, etc., to avoid having the same students move as a group every day of the school year. It provides the opportunity for students to be mixed academically and socially for instruction, which is important for the development of early adolescent students.

- **Hands-on Instruction**
  Hands-on instruction involves the actual manipulation of materials by students. Students challenged and directed by a teacher are actively engaged in their own learning.

- **IDEA '97**

  Individual with Disabilities Education Act of 1997, formerly called the Education of Handicapped Children Act (94-142); this federal law was originally passed by Congress in 1975. The law deals with the process of providing children with disabilities a free, appropriate public education. This law is reauthorized every five years.

- **IDEIA**

  Individuals with Disabilities Education Improvement Act IDEIA is the reauthorization of IDEA '97.

- **IEP**

  An *Individualized Education Program* provides a plan for specialized instruction for an individual child. IEPs for children with disabilities are developed according to the guidelines of IDEIA. Each program must be developed by a team that includes the parents or guardians.

- **Inclusion**

  Inclusion is the placement of special needs students into basic education classes on a random basis, so students can have access to the basic education program while receiving services as identified in the students' IEPs.

- **LEA**

  Local Education Agency is the school district in which the custodial parent of a child resides.

- **LRE**

  Least Restrictive Environment—Each public agency shall insure that special classes, separate schooling, or other removal of children with disabilities from the regular educational environment occurs only when the nature or severity of the disability is such that education in regular classes with the use of supplementary aides and services cannot be achieved satisfactorily.

- **Modifications**

  Modifications are changes that can be made to "what" the student is expected to learn. Modification should be considered only after all types of accommodations have been exhausted.

- **Multiple Intelligences**
  Howard Gardner's Multiple Intelligences theory is based on the idea that all humans possess the capability to learn and demonstrate new skills and concepts through a variety of senses and abilities.

- **NCLB**
  No Child Left Behind—This law is the largest federally funded program for elementary and secondary schools. Its purpose is to provide federal funds to schools with high concentrations of children living in poverty that are not achieving well academically. NCLB strengthens accountability by requiring states to implement statewide accountability systems covering all public schools and students, including children with disabilities.

- **OT**
  Occupational Therapy is therapy commonly used to develop fine motor skills.

- **PT**
  Physical Therapy is therapy commonly used to develop gross motor skills.

- **Social Equity**
  Social Equity ensures that course offerings are available to all students regardless of academic ability, social economic status, or gender.

- **Teacher Teams**
  Teacher teams are composed of teachers who each teach cooperatively. A middle school team might include teachers who instruct one of the core academic curriculum subjects, have the same students, and share a common planning period. In a middle school with an inclusion program, the intervention specialist is often assigned to a team and provides strategies and modifications for the special needs students assigned to the team. Exploratory teachers may be teamed together, so as to share the benefits of working and planning together, even though they do not share the same students or planning time.

References

Caine, R.N., & Caine, G. (1991). *Making connections: Teaching and the human brain*. Alexandria, VA: Association for Supervision and Curriculum Development.

Cotton, K, & Wikelund, K.R. (1989). *Parent Involvement in Education*. School Improvement Research Series.

Council for Exceptional Children, (2002). *Annual Report*

Desimone, L. (1999). *Linking Parent Involvement with Student Achievement: Do Race and Income Matter?* The Journal of Educational Research, 93 (1), 11–30.

Felner, R., Jackson, A., Kasak, D., Mulhall, P., Brand, S., & Flowers, N. (In press). *The impact of school reform for the middle years: A longitudinal study of a network engaged in Turning Points-based comprehensive school transformation*. In R. Takanishi & D. Hamburg (Eds.) *Preparing adolescents for the twenty-first century*. New York: Cambridge University Press.

National Commission on Excellence in Education (1983). *A Nation at Risk: The Imperative for Educational Reform*, U. S. Department of Education, Washington, D. C.

National Forum Accelerating Change in Middle Grades Education (2001). Champaign, Ill.

National Middle School Association, (2005). *This We Believe, Successful Schools for Young Adolescents*, Columbus, Ohio

United States Congress, (2004). *Individuals with Disabilities Education Improvement Act*, Public Law 108–446, Washington, D.C.

United States Congress, (2001), *No Child Left Behind, Public Law 107–110*, Washington, D.C.